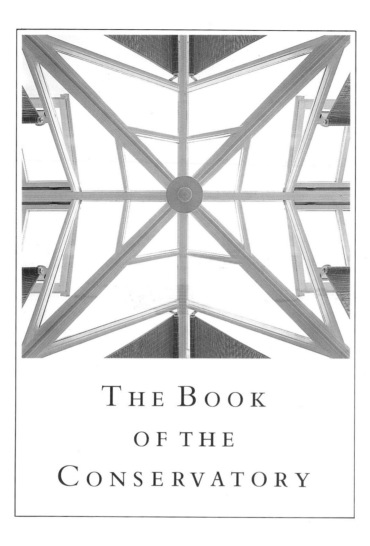

THE BOOK
OF THE
CONSERVATORY

THE BOOK
OF THE
CONSERVATORY

PETER MARSTON

WEIDENFELD & NICOLSON

LONDON

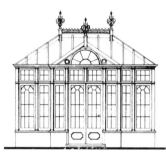

FIRST PUBLISHED IN GREAT BRITAIN IN 1992 BY
GEORGE WEIDENFELD & NICHOLSON LTD
THE ORION PUBLISHING GROUP
ORION HOUSE
5 UPPER ST MARTIN'S LANE
LONDON WC2H 9EA

PUBLISHED IN PAPERBACK IN 1995
BY GEORGE WEIDENFELD & NICOLSON LTD

PRINTED AND BOUND IN ITALY

Acknowledgements

This book originated as a result of a suggestion by Phyllis Walters. It would not, however, have taken its present form without the valuable contributions of several others.

John Miller travelled the length and breadth of England to photograph conservatories, often under extremely adverse conditions, which did not prevent him from producing outstandingly attractive pictures. Garden designer Susan Gernaey provided much useful information and help on plants for the conservatory. Josephine Marston, my partner in Marston & Langinger, researched and selected many of the beautiful illustrations. My secretary, Jackie Williams, typed and re-typed and typed again my various drafts, improving them as she went along. And, finally my wife, Rhoda, advised me on the writing of the manuscript and encouraged me throughout.

PHOTOGRAPHIC ACKNOWLEDGEMENTS

The author and publishers are grateful to the following for kind permission to reproduce illustrations:

Amdega Ltd: 105 left

A Bartholomew Ltd: 52 top, 54, (Eric Pelham) 44 right, 105 right

Bridgeman Art Library: 10, 11, 12, 104 bottom, 142

J Cockayne: 31 right, 87, 88 left

Country Living: (Alexander Bartholomew) 8–9 top

Eric Crichton: 35 bottom, 147 top, 160 bottom, 161

Christopher Dalton: 22 top

Derek Fell: 22 bottom, 24 bottom right, 68, 76, 97, 148, 150, 159 right

Copyright The Frick Collection, New York: 25

Garden Picture Library: (John Glover) 156

Historical Royal Palaces: 102–3

Francis Machin: 32, 36, 51 top, 90 left

Marianne Majerus: 135 top

Peter Marston: 31 left

Marston & Langinger: 38, 40, 41 bottom, 43, 45, 52, 53, 55 top left and right, 57 right, 58 left, 59 right, 62 bottom, 63, 71 right, 74, 77, 78, 89 bottom right, 106, 107, 109, 110–11 top, 114, 116 left, 119, 120 left and top right, 128 right, 129, 131, 137, 138 bottom and top, 139 bottom, 141 top, 143 bottom, 144 top left, 144 bottom, 160 top, 167

Peter Aprahamian 72, 89 bottom left, 89 top right, 140

Clive Boursnell 41 top, 79, 111 bottom, 116 right, 122 bottom, 126, 127, 128 left, 135 bottom, 143 top

Josephine Marston 44 bottom left, 48 bottom left, 51 bottom, 60 bottom left, 61 centre and bottom right, 67

Peter Marston 46 left, 47, 48 top, 60 top, 118

John Miller 1, 14, 23, 24 top, 26 top, 28, 29, 30 left, 37, 42 top, 43 top, 49, 50, 56, 58–9, 64, 66, 69, 75 bottom, 80–1, 84, 91, 94, 98 top, 99, 104 top, 108 right, 110 bottom, 112, 115, 117, 120, 121, 124 right, 125 left and right, 130 bottom, 132 left and right, 133 top, 133 bottom, 134 bottom, 136, 139 top, 141 bottom, 147 bottom, 151, 152, 154, 155, 157–8, 166

Dieter Pannanburg 65

Oliver Riviere 2–3, 45 top, 96

Fritz von der Schulenburg 55 bottom, 60–1, 70, 73, 82, 86, 95 top, 95 bottom, 122 top, 130, 134 top

White House Studios 75 top

John Miller: 30 right, 85 bottom

Orangeries Ltd: (Oliver Riviere) 20, 149

Courtesy of The New-York Historical Society, NYC: 21 bottom

Anthony Paine: 70–1 centre, 92

Hugh Palmer: 18, 19, 21 top, 42 bottom, 146, 157

Clay Perry: 145, 162

Pilkington plc Archives: 113

John Pipkin: 34

RHSL 26 bottom

RIBA: 33 top, 35 top, 61 top, 62 top, 101, 108 left, 124 left

RIBA Drawings Collection: 24 bottom left

RIBA Library: 21 centre, 27, 33 bottom, 123

Royal Commission for Historical Monuments: 98 right, 100

Fritz von der Schulenburg: 85 top, 98 bottom, 127 bottom

May Woods: 16–17

World Press Network: 93

Contents

INTRODUCTION

OPPOSITE *The conservatory in* The Water Babies *by Charles Kingsley (1863), as painted by Albert Goodwin. The setting, with camellias fan-grown against the wall, Victorian flowerpots of geranium cuttings, and a roof shaded by several grapevines is very pleasing.*

LEFT *Design for the interior of the Prince of Wales's conservatory at Carlton House – an impressive, glazed fantasy based on Tudor fan-vaulting in wood, not stone. It, in all probability, would have been unbuildable.*

Most people think of a conservatory as a place for the preservation of tender plants, but for the majority of owners today – since the eighteenth century in fact, when glass ceased to be a luxury, and large windows and glazed roofs became feasible – they are much more. Glasshouses may originally have been synonymous with green-houses but, as the enthusiastic travellers of the Enlightenment returned with exotic specimens to propagate at home, the conserva-tory became a room for people as well as plants, a setting for enjoying the pleasures of the outdoors while sheltered from wind and rain, and a natural transition between house and garden. As soon as the risk of frost passed, the citrus fruit and other tender plants in

The Luncheon in the Conservatory, *by Louise Abbema (1877). The plants have been hauled aside, a carpet thrown down on the floor, and a table brought into a conservatory to make room for a luncheon party. Note the pretty painted side table used for plates and a glass.*

tubs and pots were turned out of the classical eighteenth-century orangeries to decorate the terrace so the buildings could be used for entertaining within the garden. Tables would be set up inside and laid for supper parties; on summer evenings guests would admire the broad views through the huge sash windows and french doors. The popularity of orangeries spread not just through the cooler parts of Europe – Sweden, Holland, Germany, Northern France, and England – but to America as well. Noteworthy conservatories and orangeries began to be built in America in the eighteenth century, including, of course, the famous example at Mount Vernon, constructed in the 1770s.

As the Industrial Age advanced, developments in the technique of casting and building with iron, together with cheaper glass, made possible increasingly delicate and fanciful structures. For the first time in the history of architecture, the relative proportions of the fabric of buildings could be altered, allowing glass to become the dominant element. This coincided, as the frontiers of the known world expanded, with the discovery of countless completely new plants. By the early nineteenth century, the construction of conservatories was well enough advanced for private enthusiasts, as well as the expert gardeners of large estates, to be able to conserve and grow the rarest specimens far from their tropical origins. The private conservatory, or winter garden, was recognized by Victorian writers and painters as a background for romance, a spot where lovers could withdraw for a tête-à-tête behind the potted palms. The public conservatory, such as the great crystal palaces built out of hundreds of tons of glass as architectural halls, first in London in 1851 and then in New York, were monuments to the ambitions and progress of the age. As visitors in medieval times wandered amazed through the great Gothic cathedrals, so Victorian promenaders marvelled at these extravagant creations whose delicate frameworks, likewise in full view, could support arches and vaulting of such grandeur. A marriage of technology and art, of the urge to live outdoors and the desire to keep the outdoors within manageable limits, the conservatory represents the achievements and aspirations of the nineteenth century.

As a room for entertaining of all kinds, from tea parties to balls, the conservatory survived into the languorous Edwardian times. But as garden rooms became popular with the middle as well as the upper classes, they were added to smaller and smaller houses and gradually fell out of favour with the rich and fashionable. By the Twenties, the conservatory had almost disappeared; few new ones were built and existing ones frequently fell into disrepair and were pulled down. There was also a reaction against their relative lack of comfort. When central heating and fitted carpets made the rest of the house warm all year around, a conservatory that was cold in winter – or prohibitively expensive to heat – seemed a quaint, impractical relic, out of place in a modern, efficient age. For the next fifty years little interest was taken in them. Indeed, when I started the company that is now Marston & Langinger in the early 1970s, the idea of the conservatory had so far retreated from public consciousness that I kept having to explain that we did not build music schools!

But, just as new methods of production and engineering made the conservatory possible, more recent ones have made it practical. The re-awakened interest in conservatories reflects the awareness that new types of glazing, heating, and ventilation have made glass rooms as safe and comfortable as rooms of brick and stone. The conservatory is now seen as an addition to one's home that can be put to any

number of uses — dining room, sitting room, poolhouse, study. While plants are, of course, still an important aspect of these rooms, they are no longer the original impulse behind them. People now build conservatories so they can have a room filled with more natural light than a conventional room, especially one in a period home of few and little windows.

Before it can be enjoyed, however, the conservatory today presents the homeowner with numerous problems and uncertainties. For instance, though the structure of the conservatory will be made principally of glass, it is the framework that will give it a distinctive character, and materials and style must be carefully chosen to make the addition compatible with the house. The unique character of the conservatory must also be taken into consideration when it is decorated. Too often conservatories are furnished in the same manner as the other rooms of the house, without regard to their special indoor-outdoor nature, and they may end up looking slightly ridiculous, as if some mistake has been made in giving a sitting room transparent walls. Finally, planting in the conservatory should take into account the requirements of different species for temperature, space, and light, the compatibility of the plants with one another and with the way the room is used and decorated.

If this survey of conservatories through the ages in Britain and America, covering examples from immense classical orangeries to tiny cottage glasshouses, inspires you to commission your own crystal palace, this book will also guide you through the best ways of designing, furnishing and planting it. In any case, however, I hope you will be as impressed as I have been by the extraordinary results that can be achieved by building with glass.

LEFT *The inside of this decaying orangery is now used for growing marrows and potatoes. The terracotta pots and camellias planted against the door columns are a reminder of its grander past.*

OVERLEAF *Built in front of evergreens, box, yew and laurel, the light lichen-covered stone and white painted woodwork of this orangery at Pythouse, Wiltshire, make a good contrast with the setting throughout the year. The simple design, decorated with flat pilasters, a portico and an urn finial, makes the most of the commanding position. Stone balls similar to those on the steps which rise up the bank of wild daffodils have replaced the original urns on the solid stone balustrade. Concealed behind this lies a glass roof, and the interior, little used, has recently been repainted white.*

PART I

The Conservatory From the Outside

THE EVOLUTION OF AN IDEA

EARLY ORANGERIES
AND CONSERVATORIES

The aristocracy's interest in horticulture at the end of the seventeenth century and a more scientific approach to cultivation led to the construction of the first orangeries and conservatories to over-winter tender plants. It is hard to understand today the excitement produced by germinating seeds and growing cuttings from the Mediterranean, the West Indies and India, and the luxury of being able to pick a fresh orange, lemon, or pineapple straight from the plants for the table. The earliest buildings were used simply to keep the frost from plants so that they would survive until they could be grown again outdoors in the spring. Later, heat was added with timber or 'sea-coal'-fired stoves. Gardeners then found that, by adding large windows, specimens could not only be kept alive but induced to grow well during the cold months of the year. The result was that buildings were constructed in the classical style, with broad windows filling the spaces between the columns, but with solid roofs, an adaptation of the classic orders which still works well today. The architectural style developed quickly, and the fashionable enthusiasm for exotic gardening soon produced some extravagant structures; by 1704 Queen Anne was commissioning a large greenhouse for Kensington Palace. The design by Hawksmoor and Vanbrugh, an elaborate, substantial brick structure with tall sash windows and a slate roof, has a richly decorated exterior, though a not entirely satisfactory appearance. The interior, brightly lit and decorated with beautiful Grinling Gibbons carvings, was furnished with fine statuary set in niches along the walls and provided space to conserve hundreds of orange trees

ABOVE *It is quite possible to grow pineapples under glass, and they can be started from a specimen bought at the greengrocer.*

OPPOSITE *The large conservatory built by Messenger & Co. for Thomas Cook, the travel agent, at Sennowe Park, Devon.*

during the winter. The orangery became a requirement of grand houses, and examples from the early eighteenth century exist all over England. These early buildings have survived in the grounds of great houses in Britain and all over Europe, whilst the later, more vulnerable, all-glass and timber or iron buildings of Victorian and Edwardian construction, that require so much more maintenance, have, in most cases, perished.

The usual plan of orangeries was a rectangular or a grander, semi-circular arrangement, with a central pavilion. They were generally constructed of brick clad with stone and facing south. Their floor-length sash windows were often large enough for the lower sash to be raised high enough to walk through, thereby avoiding doors, which would be of an inappropriately small scale for the building. The glazing was divided with a framework of round columns or flat pilasters and supported a classical entablature. The roof would generally be hidden from view, and, as Gertrude Jekyll put it, 'veiled with a handsome balustrade'. The citrus trees, camellias, and other plants over-wintered in orangeries were planted in large pots, or tubs, the bigger ones of the Versailles type, with brackets for sliding poles through so that they could be lifted by two or more men. In summer, when the trees and shrubs were moved out onto the terrace, the emptied orangery provided a fine room for parties and entertainments — Queen Anne referred to hers as a 'summer supper house'. Later examples were used for ballrooms, and a number were built, as late as Edwardian times, specially for that purpose. The son of the travel agent Thomas Cook, while travelling in the Far

RIGHT *Elevation of Sheringham Hall (now Park) by Humphrey Repton, 1816. The glasshouse is of classical design but has the more horticulturally practical glass roof that became usual at about this time.*

LEFT *The Elgin Botanic Gardens, Manhattan, 1825. A conservatory modelled on a southern plantation house on the site today covered by Rockefeller Center.*

RIGHT *A turn-of-the-century photograph of the extraordinarily exotic roofs on the conservatories at Alton Towers, Staffordshire.*

BELOW *Orangery, Dumbarton Oaks, Washington DC. This grand orangery, at the mansion where the 1944 Allied Conference that originated the United Nations was held, is set in a garden designed by the landscape gardener Beatrix Farrand. Although it has a solid roof, the interior is illuminated by three bays of windows on each side of central glazed doors.*

East in the early 1900s, wrote to his architects in England commissioning a glass ballroom for his house at Sennow Park; the conservatory company Messengers finished the building for his return.

Plants grown in an orangery with a glazed front and sides and solid back and roof suffer from straining towards the light. This was not such a problem at first, with plants being moved out into the open in April or May, but, as more plants were introduced, and all-year-round indoor gardening became established, it became imperative to glaze the roof. Many of the first orangeries were converted to glass roofs during the

nineteenth century, not always very success-fully in architectural terms. Orangeries of the late eighteenth and early nineteenth century were designed with glass roofs, among them the one at Alton Towers in Staffordshire, with its series of eccentric decorated domes, and that at Syon in Midd-lesex. The buildings in the gardens of Syon House, by Charles Fowler, built between 1820 and 1827, consist of a central domed pavilion linked with two quadrant arcades ending in matching pavilions. While having a formal plan and classical sandstone façade, the central pavilion has a tall, ten-metre-diameter cast- and wrought-iron dome sup-ported internally on twelve cast-iron columns. The building was recently restored and the now clean, impressively light and delicate dome contrasts strikingly with the solid structure beneath. While the great iron conservatories were developed in the last century, classical orangeries continued to be built as garden buildings and later as museums, galleries, and even banking halls. In this century they have been used as restaurants and, more recently, as swimming-pool enclosures, overcoming the architectural problem of designing large single-storey additions to period property. The arrangement of columns filled in with

The impressive range of conservatories at Syon House, Middlesex. Their design forms a transition between the stone buildings of the eighteenth century and the wrought- and cast-iron designs of the nineteenth century. The recent restoration and cleaning reveal the full beauty of the extraordinarily fine glazing in the dome.

RIGHT *Colney Hall,
Norfolk. A rather grand
wood-and-stucco façade in
front of a plain ridged roof.
The orangery now houses a
Victorian fernery complete
with a pool and tufa dripping
with moss and small ferns.*

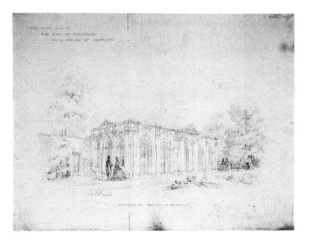

ABOVE *Perspective sketch by Matthew Digby Wyatt, of
Fern House at Ashridge for the Earl of Brownlow, 1864.*

RIGHT *The Orangery at Conestoga House, Lancaster,
Pennsylvania. The simple building, with its solid roof, owes its
effect to the grand, semi-circular-headed orangery sash windows.
These are partioned into very small panes and painted a soft
greenish-grey. At the front of the windows are oleanders with
pink double flowers, plumbago, red fuchsias, and small,
unclipped box trees.*

large, decorative glazing with a substantial internal cornice and a glazed or lead-covered, boarded, or plastered ceiling makes a beautiful and impressive room. With a lower proportion of glazing, and their generally greater height than timber and metal conservatories, orangeries are easy to keep cool in summer, and, double-glazed with coated glass, may be used throughout the year, requiring no more heating than conventional buildings.

INNOVATION IN THE VICTORIAN AGE

All the great, technically daring nineteenth-century glass buildings are based on iron construction, using a mixture of cast and wrought iron. The two most important figures of this era are John Claudius Loudon (1783–1843) and Sir Joseph Paxton (1803–65). Both started as gardeners, and both developed new methods of construction, prompted by contemporary ideas of the best way to let the maximum amount of light through glass roofs onto plants, and thereby grow the largest and most exotic specimens. At the beginning of the last century, gardeners thought it was essential for light to shine through glass at an angle as close to ninety degrees from the surface of the pane as possible; this theory inspired much debate about the ideal shape for a roof. Loudon developed the curvilinear design which could be seen on the roofs of many buildings of the 1820s and '30s – at Bicton Park in Devon, the central dome at Syon House, the Great Palm house at Kew (by Decimus Burton and Richard Turner), and Dallam Towers in Cumbria. The theory was that, by curving the surface of the glass, the rays of the sun would always strike a part of the roof at the correct angle regardless of time or season.

Paxton's approach achieved the same result with a series of ridges and furrows,

RIGHT *Curvilinear Conservatory, from* The Greenhouse Companion *by J. C. Loudon. This type of conservatory, built against a house wall, was heated by a stove behind the wall and by the flue running up through it. Ventilators are set in the bottom of the base wall.*

which also stiffened the structure. The most exciting results of his ideas were the magnificent glass buildings at Chatsworth in Derbyshire, including the Great Conservatory, and the Crystal Palace for the 1851 Exhibition in London. Neither exists now; the Great Conservatory was demolished in 1920 with the help of dynamite in the post-war spirit of economy, and the Crystal Palace was destroyed by fire in 1934 (much of it was not crystal, or glass, but wood). The inventiveness of these men, coupled with the developments of such builders and architects as Decimus Burton and Richard Turner and the relative cheapness of iron and glass, created a new industry. Glass buildings of every size were put up, not just as greenhouses, but as railway stations, museums, and shopping arcades. In Europe and America, the Crystal Palace was particularly influential in creating the fashion, and in 1853 the New York Crystal Palace Exhibition Hall was completed using Paxton's method of construction but exceeding his greatest span, with a huge 23-metre (76-foot)-high dome at the intersection of two large aisles; it, too, was destroyed by fire, in 1858.

Loudon, an energetic Scot, built up a large nursery in Hackney catering for the contemporary passion for exotics, and, with a keen interest in tender plants, developed a method of constructing curved lean-tos and domed glass structures using thin, wroughtiron glazing bars of great delicacy. On domed roofs the quantity of bars was progressively reduced by jointing them as they rose towards the summit, so eight would become four, and four two, and eventually one, resulting in a structurally sophisticated, rigid 'skin', like the metal surface of a modern car, which forms a stiff shell, despite being thin enough to cut with shears. The glasshouses created by this technique, adopted and developed by the building company W. & D. Bailey, were severely beautiful; their simple structure and absence of superfluous decoration give them a quality more usually associated with twentieth-century architecture.

New ways of using wrought iron for the important structural members made possible the construction of very large domes.

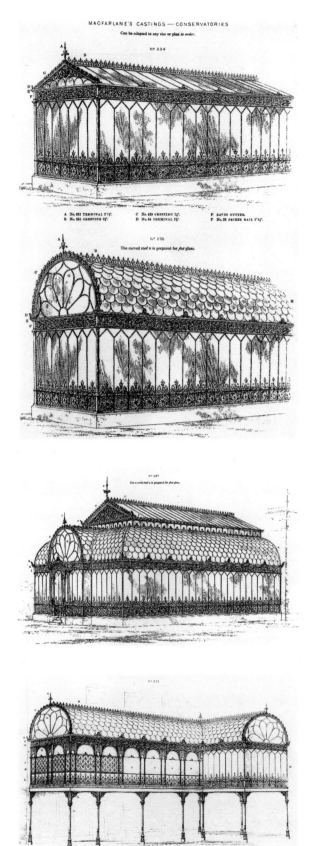

OPPOSITE, The Palm House built for Lady Rolle at Bicton Hall in Devon by W. & D. Bailey. The building is constructed against a rear wall and consists of a tall semi-circular central dome with two quarter-round domes at the sides. One of the best surviving glasshouses based on a system of construction devised by the gardener John Loudon during the early nineteenth century.

LEFT Examples by Macfarlane's of standard components assembled into conservatories of intricate design with elaborate decoration.

When the Palm House, one of the biggest glass buildings of its day, was built at Kew in 1844, newly developed rolled and bent 'I' section wrought-iron girders enabled it to be 19.8 metres (66 feet) high with no internal columns – a masterpiece of engineering. This was possible because of the nature of wrought iron, which can be rolled and worked into shapes, such as great curved girders, while remaining very strong and highly resistant to fracture. It has now been replaced by mild steel, which is less expensive to produce and more suitable for rolling into the standard sections used today.

Cast iron, more than any other material, typifies nineteenth-century engineering and construction. From crude early experiments in the eighteenth century, such as the famous

Reconstructed conservatory at the Horniman Museum in south London, originally built for that family's house in Coombe Cliff, Croydon. This magnificent conservatory constructed by the Glasgow ironfounders Macfarlane's fell into disrepair when the ownership of the house passed to the local authority. Having been painstakingly dismantled, cleaned, and repaired, it languished for a number of years before a grant from English Heritage gave it a new home a few miles away, next to the Horniman Museum of Ethnographia.

bridge at Coalbrookdale, the craft developed rapidly, and by the mid-nineteenth century, great technical virtuosity was being achieved at very low cost. It was used on a vast scale for everything from small domestic goods to major engineering feats such as

the manufacture of standardized products, which in turn could be mass-marketed by magazine and newspaper advertisements for the makers' illustrated catalogues. From the middle of the century iron founders offered complete ranges of castings for all-cast-iron

the great railway stations or the Crystal Palace. The latter would not have been possible without the cast-iron columns and framework, cleverly assembled with ingenious knuckle joints which were made fast with metal wedges. Its numerous identical cast-iron components, arranged in a modular system, enabled it to be designed and constructed in less than a year. With the growth of nineteenth-century industrialization, cast iron became more and more popular. It was ideal for factory- and workshop-based batch production and for

conservatories that could be assembled in different ways, rather like Lego, to make buildings of every conceivable size and shape. Annotated engravings of sample buildings showed how an entire structure might be put together from the various numbered parts. As Victorian taste developed, so the catalogues grew larger, with a profusion of decorative castings for columns, pilasters, panels, braces and brackets, finials and crestings, staging, floor grilles and heaters becoming available to provide decorative detail.

But although in many ways an excellent material, cast iron can suffer from rust and frost damage. The metalwork requires constant, thorough repainting to prevent rust unless the components are galvanized (dipped in hot zinc) after they are made, a process that was rarely used. Frost has been the greatest enemy of cast-iron buildings, causing the most structural damage. Water, seeping into fractures that inevitably result from settlement, poor design, or inferior manufacture, expands when it freezes in winter, opening cracks, forcing the components apart, and allowing more water in to rust the exposed surfaces. As a result, rela-

tively few of the great cast-iron buildings more than a hundred years old have survived. Those that have are generally important public buildings for which the funds for maintenance have been more readily and consistently available. Cast iron is still used in quantity today, but its cost, maintenance requirements, and the general decline of the craft limit its use, particularly externally. Nowadays cast aluminium provides a good substitute because, although not so stiff, it is much lighter, suffers little corrosion, and, most important, is unlikely to fracture. It

can be painted or stove enamelled and is reasonably cheap to produce. (It is, therefore, surprising that it is not used more often.) Aluminium also allows the free use of Victorian decoration, as there is little more expense involved in making a decorative component than a plain one.

The widest use of aluminium today is for buildings constructed from aluminium-alloy extrusions with a stove-enamelled paint finish, a system of design that is easy to make weather-tight and requires little maintenance but that offers little flexibility for the

ABOVE *An elaborate two-storey octagonal design constructed entirely of cast aluminium. The extensive decoration is made affordable by using a limited number of castings ingeniously repeated throughout the structure.*

ABOVE, LEFT *A charming metal lean-to greenhouse in a cottage garden. The serpentine shape of the roof eliminates the need for front windows or a gutter.*

The curved shape of this timber-and-aluminium conservatory at Hatfield House, designed in 1990 by Francis Machin, makes a bold silhouette amongst the trees in this fine setting. The double curvature of the roof, which in glass would be prohibitively expensive, is here achieved with facets glazed with flexed clear polycarbonate plastic.

designer, or facility for delicate detail. Aluminium extrusions are most commonly used for public buildings, such as glass-covered shopping malls or municipal swimming-pools, although there are several conservatory manufacturers offering all-aluminium buildings. Aluminium extrusion roofs, however, are common and are frequently combined with timber framework and windows and doors.

CONSERVATORIES FOR EVERYMAN

Most conservatories of the late-Victorian and Edwardian periods were constructed of timber and glass, the exceptions being the grander buildings made of cast or wrought iron or stone. Timber was readily available; it could easily be worked, cut, joined, and even steam-bent for curved roofs, and, combined with iron-and-steel reinforcement, could be used to make large, strong, and light structures. Late-nineteenth-century engineers were particularly good at combining metal and timber in unified designs to produce strong buildings with an attractive, decorative effect by adding, for example, lacy cast-iron braces to the roof trusses. Dozens of companies, many of them with substantial factories and large work-forces, competed with more and more elaborate designs to supply what had become the necessary adjunct of the Victorian and Edwardian villa.

By the turn of the century, the most ambitious styles in wood were being offered, incorporating every feature possible – fan-lights, roof lanterns, projecting gables, round bays, porches, mixtures of curved and flat roofs with valleys, hips, and gables, all decorated with brackets, columns, layers of mouldings, fancy metalwork, fretted timber, and turned finials. Bizarre styles sprang up, such as Tudor half-timbered, which might be combined with a Japanese look. Striving to be more impressive and exotic, designers produced Bavarian hunting-lodge conservatories or glass Swiss cottages. The general decline into fussiness and vulgarity and the maintenance level required by the

method of construction combined to make conservatories go out of fashion around the time of the First World War, sadly causing some of the best buildings to be abandoned or demolished, among them Paxton's Great Stove House at Chatsworth. The eclipse lasted fifty years, until changing attitudes to the restoration and adaptation of period property, combined with the decline of modernism, led to a revival. Although some notable developments have been made in metal buildings, particularly the use of extruded and cast aluminium, the majority of conservatories are now built of wood.

Most conservatories are built as extensions to existing houses, and it is generally important that the new blend with the old. Timber is ideal for this – it is suited to a domestic scale, can be finished to match existing woodwork or combined with stone

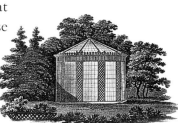

ABOVE *Vignette from* Observations on the Theory & Practice of Landscape Gardening, *H. Repton, 1805. This pavilion in the form of a fully glazed greenhouse is interesting for its treillage decoration.*

Plan

Octagon

Conservatory

Lobby

House

PLATE Nº 9

A·TWO·STOREYED·CONSERVATORY· ❋ ·Constructed·on·the·Patent·System·of·Messenger·&·Cº·Horticultural·Builders·Loughborough· ❋ ·by·E·W·Godwin·F·S·A·

LEFT *A speculative design from a catalogue by conservatory builders Messenger & Co. By the end of Queen Victoria's reign, conservatories were being offered in an extraordinary range of architectural styles. This grotesque mixture of influences is an example of the sort of building that caused respected architects of the early years of this century to disapprove of conservatories and contributed to their decline.*

33

or brickwork, and, more than other materials, is suited to individual designs, essential when the work must match the scale and details of features on the house. It does, however, have limits. Although perfect for the construction of roofs, it does not make a good seal for roof glazing, nor will it support the weight of workmen climbing onto the roof for maintenance. The problems can, however, be simply overcome by using low-maintenance metal or plastic capping over the joints of the glass, and having these finished to match the appearance of the woodwork.

The timber generally chosen in the past for conservatories of all-wood construction was Scandinavian deal, or Scots pine, which has been used for hundreds of years for ordinary windows, doors, floors, and roofs. Douglas fir, grown in western America, is stronger, straighter, and accepts paint well. Pitch pine, from the United States, was popular from the mid-nineteenth century for more vulnerable components, such as sills and timber gutters, but is no longer as common. It is a very strong, dense, and oily timber which does not take oil-bound paint well, but is long-lasting. Burmese teak, hard and durable as iron but expensive, has been used for more than a century for important buildings. Usually painted to protect and seal putty glazing, it can be left to weather naturally, and a number of buildings, particularly in the 1970s, have been constructed of clear-finished teak. A cheaper alternative is cedar, from the West Coast of the United States and Canada, which can also be clear-finished and is naturally resistant to insect and fungus attack. Its main drawback is its weakness, making thick supporting members necessary, and softness, making it difficult to mould and finish finely. It is, however,

in general use for greenhouse manufacture, and a number of conservatories of lighter construction are also built with it. Top-quality painted conservatories are also built in timbers of the mahogany type such as lauan and utile, from the Philippines and West Africa respectively. These timbers are very strong and durable and can be finely finished and take paint well, but are more expensive to buy and work. Occasionally

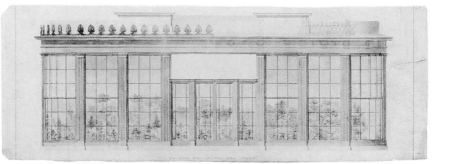

35

materials such as oak, previously restricted to sills and thresholds, are used for decorative effect. Generally from North America, oak has the advantage of coming from managed and sustainable sources.

Since conservatories are built to protect and nurture plants, it would be ironic, to say

The curious design of this glasshouse (which collapsed in 1987) contrasts with the elegant formality of the surrounding parterre, and the house it adjoined. The curved shape is made up of a series of facets which create a pleasing pattern of reflections. The conservatory was entered from the house through a sash window converted into a door, and was used to house an enormous vine.

the least, for them to be built of timber from a country whose forests have been ruthlessly depleted – a cause for serious concern. The growing population and domestic demand in Third World countries, coupled with their continued supply of traditional markets in Europe, has resulted in a rapid increase in the pace of deforestation in India, Sri Lanka, Africa, the Philippines, Malaya, Central America, and, more recently, in South America. North America, the Scandinavian countries, and a few Asian and African states do have managed forests, and their timber may be bought with a clear conscience. However, it is as well to seek assurances, if a conservatory is built in

timber, that the wood has come from properly managed sources, so that no trees are felled without new trees being planted to replace them in good time.

Whatever the tree and its source, timber needs to be seasoned and finished properly, so that it will, properly maintained, last for a hundred years or more; there are many two- or three-hundred-year-old houses with original sash windows constructed of softwood, of the slenderest sections, without preservative treatment, that have survived with no more than regular repainting. Virtually all timber used externally with glazing needs some sort of finishing, not just to preserve it and make it weathertight, but to improve its appearance. The material used can be varnish, stain, or clear paint (which is really a varnish with the additional body of opaque pigments), or seals, which can also be clear or stained, that penetrate the timber and retain the surface texture. No matter what the finish – varnish, seal, or paint – all require, contrary to popular belief, regular refinishing every three to ten years, depending on the location of building, the type of timber, and the finish used (three to five years is the most typical). There are many claims made by paint manufacturers for their products, but, as with soap powders, no specific lists of ingredients or guarantees. The subject is also obfuscated by marketing terms such as microporous, which all paints are to varying degrees. Until recently most paints were a mixture of white lead zinc oxide or red lead with linseed oil, pigments, and an oxidizing agent to make the paint harden quickly. This paint was, and still is, of good quality, and can be very durable, but must be applied to properly dried timber, as it is not particularly elastic and will tend to crack and flake as the moisture within the

timber rises to the surface and the joints open. Lead-based paint has largely disappeared through the cost of manufacture and public concern over its toxicity, to be replaced by alkyd paints, which recently have been much improved, with a number of manufacturers producing special exterior woodwork grades. These are more expensive, but much more durable.

There are also large numbers of water-based stains which are easy to prepare and to recoat, as they tend to powder rather than flake with age, so the woodwork does not need tedious sanding before recoating, and have the greatest claim for longevity – up to ten years. However, they are not without

problems: they suffer from blocking – that is, a tendency to stay slightly tacky, which means windows and doors can stick – and they are not suitable for use over metal without special primers, do not adhere to some glazing compounds, and only a few brands enable a high decorative finish to be achieved. The general conclusion is that either oil-based paint or a carefully selected water-based paint probably make the best finish for timber conservatories, but the highest quality, specifically formulated for exterior woodwork, should be used. After all, the cost of paint is insignificant when compared with the cost of preparing and applying it.

A conservatory recently built to make the most of the views across a Kent valley without blocking the aspect from the first-floor rooms. The overall height has been kept to a minimum by dividing the roof into three hipped lanterns. Though made of timber, the building is based on a classical orangery using the Doric order, with pilasters and pedestals. It is double glazed and well heated to provide a garden room for year-round use.

2

PERIOD STYLE

TAILORING THE DESIGN

Many people contemplating a new conservatory have no choice about where it can be built, particularly in a city, where space is more likely to be limited and where the new room might fulfil an essential role as a dining room, sitting room, or perhaps a link between rooms. For a suburban or country house, the choice of location can be more complicated. There may be a number of alternative sites, and, if the conservatory adjoins a large garden, the outside aspect will matter much more. The simplest and most desirable location is always the one that offers the greatest freedom for design. This is likely to be an open site, where the building will be free-standing, or possibly, attached to a wall; in any case, it must be related to the garden design as a whole, with consideration given to the right planting and terracing. People who live in conservation areas may be hampered by planning restrictions. This is more likely to arise if the house is an important or listed building, in which case the local planning officers will take a keen interest, especially if the proposed conservatory will be tall or built on to a roof. To minimize problems, it is always best to consult the authorities at an early stage.

OPPOSITE *This south-facing, bay-ended conservatory in Bungay, Suffolk, leads off the drawing room to fit neatly between the house and the river. It hides from the garden the utility room, an earlier addition.*

IN THE COUNTRY

Most of the earliest buildings, the orangeries of the eighteenth century, were built in the gardens of grand estates as summerhouses, to over-winter precious and tender plants and to enhance the view of the gardens from the main house. In this respect they sometimes had a role as a folly, but with some practical uses – to provide a focus for the eye in a landscape that was regarded rather like the painter's canvas, or to obscure a utilitarian part of the garden or an unsightly view of the adjoining estate. Most designers sought to produce a balanced garden plan with avenues, terraces, balustrades, parterres,

OPPOSITE, BELOW *Designed and built by Marston & Langinger in 1980 for a country house near Inverness, this conservatory has been carefully made to look as if it were added around the time the house was built, although it is double-glazed and the roof glass is secured with aluminium fillets rather than putty. It leads from the drawing room and has wonderful views of the surrounding estate and the loch and mountains beyond.*

fountains, and pools, in which the orangery was only part of the overall scheme. In general, orangeries were built at the back of a terrace onto which the trees and shrubs in tubs and pots could be removed from the glasshouse for the summer. They were often sited in front of trees, particularly evergreens, where they would mask the lower, less satisfactory part of the aspect and provide contrast to the dark foliage. Many were positioned at the end of avenues or at intersecting walkways, to provide a pleasant distraction for promenaders turning a corner. They also offered a resting place during garden walks, and were used as refreshment pavilions for visitors being shown around the grounds, as they often are today at houses open to the public. Their original role as summerhouse, designed for eating and entertaining in a garden setting, meant it was impractical to site them too far from the main house.

As the orangery ceased to be regarded as a kind of garden pavilion, and as its role as a special kind of reception or living room developed, permanent furnishing was introduced, and access to the house became more important. Owners wanted to be able to walk with their guests directly and under cover to their garden rooms to show off their

collection of exotics. Georgian architecture posed a particular difficulty in this respect as making an addition at a different scale, in a somewhat different style, would have ruined the symmetry of the house. The usual solution was to set the orangery slightly apart from the main house and to connect them with an arcade, or, later, a glazed link. In this way, possibly balancing the arrangement with domestic buildings on the opposite side of the house, the integrity of the architecture of the house itself remained unimpaired. There are many examples of later orangeries built on one of the rear corners of the house, possibly as one of a pair of pavilions, linked with the house by either a straight or a curved glazed corridor. The rear wall of the corridor often provided the practical advantage of masking coach houses and stables, built alongside, making them invisible from the terrace (an arrangement that works particularly well for poolhouses now).

By Regency times, not only the walls but the roofs of glasshouses were glazed, and conservatories had become accepted as part of the house. Verandas were in vogue; they usually had concave copper roofs that weathered to beautiful verdigris, a colour then very much in fashion. Some were built around the house, sometimes on all four sides, with glazed rooves that did not block the light into the reception rooms, so people gradually became accustomed to glass extensions of their homes. It was simply a matter of time before the sides of verandas were glazed over as well, and extended into conservatories that led directly from the sitting or drawing room. The appeal of being able to sit in a bright room, naturally warmed, even in winter, by the greenhouse effect of light through the glazed roof, was

BELOW *This conservatory has been designed to make a pretty everyday room leading from the kitchen at the side of this fine period house and to mask the view of extensions and outbuildings.*

immediately apparent, and architectural pattern books of the day show charming designs for villas with delicate classical conservatories attached to them. These were usually painted to imitate stone or bronze.

The Victorian Conservatory

By the 1830s a new style of architecture had developed which would set the pattern for the next hundred years. Romantic revivals of the medieval gothic and the picturesque – the *cottage orné* – required an asymmetrical approach to the design of houses. There was great interest in the old vernacular buildings, timber framed and thatched, or with brick

LEFT *A substantial bay-ended conservatory built by Marston & Langinger for a Victorian Gothic house on a Surrey hillside. It has numerous doors which can be folded back to make the most of the magnificent view across the Weald below. The decorative features on the building have been carefully matched to those on the house.*

RIGHT *This conservatory, near Grantham, Lincolnshire, built as part of the renovations of a rambling, early nineteenth-century house, fills a space created by three walls. The owners asked Marston & Langinger to design a conservatory as an extension to their kitchen, in a style appropriate for their architecturally listed home. A projecting gable adds interest and focus to the lean-to design. The absence of horizontal glazing bars and the use of narrow vertical panes is typical of the early nineteenth century, only here single units of toughened double-glazing have been used.*

RIGHT *Typical mid-Victorian glasshouses at Netherbyrnes, Scotland. The lean-to in the foreground is more of a working greenhouse and was probably constructed to house a vine which would have been trained to cover the large roof interior. In the background, the conservatory built for ornamental plants and reflecting the Victorian sense of order is taller and has more elaborate windows, cast-iron cresting and a finial, and, at the corners, stone piers surmounted by carved urns. Both conservatories are glazed with tiny panes of overlapping horticultural-grade glass. The landscaping surrounding the buildings has evolved with time, and the general effect, with a mixture of formality and informality and planting right up to the buildings, is very attractive.*

and clay pantile roofing. The architect John Nash's designs for simple houses or cottages, with gables and chimneys, porches, lead-light windows and overhanging eaves are typical of the period. The method of design imitating the natural organic growth of old building dictated by need rather than a plan, with symmetrically arranged rooms and

features, lent itself particularly to the addition of a conservatory. Throughout the Victorian period, conservatories were used to balance the design of the houses, tucked into corners, extending from gables, or wings, constructed in material and style, often strongly contrasting with the rest, but reinforcing the sense of naturalism, free of classical discipline. As a well-known conservatory manufacturer of late-Victorian times, Messenger & Co., put it,

It is a remarkable circumstance, that our conservatories, the caskets in which we keep the highest works of art we possess – nature's art – our flowers, should so long have remained so inartistic, so unworthy to set off their jewels. It is with a view to attempt to bear our part in remedying this long-standing insult to the flowers, that we issue these designs. There has been little demand for artistic conservatories, and consequently there is no great supply. However, we think the tide is turning and art seems about to be released from her prison within the four walls of the house, and to assert her influence and charm over our gardens.

This appeared in the foreword to the company's catalogue, entitled 'Artistic Conservatories'. By that time many other firms were building conservatories in every conceivable size and style. The conservatory became so familiar and accepted that by the 1880s it was not unusual for a large and elaborate iron glasshouse to be built – for instance, as a ballroom – leading directly off the main façade of the house.

The Victorians liked to heat their conservatories. It was a matter of ambition and pride to be able to grow and display the most exotic, rare, and tender plants and then to be able to take tea amongst them. They invented the idea of the conservatory as the floral sitting room for eating dainty sandwiches, for gossip, and for the young to make assignations amongst the palms. Accordingly, their garden rooms were placed next to the library or the drawing room, or perhaps the entrance hall, but never the kitchen. They also had relatively little connection with the garden outside, unlike earlier buildings and those constructed today. Many Georgian orangeries were equipped with façades of double doors or windows which could be raised high enough to walk through. Contemporary buildings are usually fitted with pairs of large double doors that can be opened out and folded back during the summer months and lead onto a terrace. Victorian buildings were conceived as crystal bell jars to contain and protect an exotic environment within. They certainly had doors, perhaps a pair leading down into the garden, and a rear single door as well for the gardener and his barrow, but these were relatively unimportant and generally regarded as an interruption to the design of the building.

Contemporary Conservatories

The majority of conservatories are built onto the house, but a few free-standing ones are constructed, often as ornamental glasshouses, particularly in situations where a greenhouse is required, and must be on view because of the constraints of the site. If a new house is being built, take advantage, at planning stage, of incorporating the special space a conservatory offers into the layout of the reception rooms. For example, if the general plan is U-shaped, the central courtyard can be used as a glass-roofed atrium, providing a link between the ground-floor rooms as well as a large room for entertaining. Conservatories are now widely as-

sociated with eating and drinking, and are commonly used as informal dining rooms for breakfast, tea, or cocktails. Not surprisingly they often adjoin the kitchen, frequently connected by an opening in the exterior wall of the kitchen. Quite apart from social reasons, this would not have been feasible for the Victorians because they were restricted to draughty single-glazing in small panes, and suffered the associated condensation problems of uninsulated buildings. Another difference in the use of conservatories is that they are now regarded much

ABOVE *This Warwickshire conservatory, designed by Marston & Langinger in 1989, follows the same architectural principles as the house but at a reduced scale and with contrasting materials. It has a main, gabled roof on the same axis, with a projecting gable echoing those on the house. The base walls incorporate panels salvaged from other alterations to the house.*

BELOW *The conservatory in this design uses three existing walls and features an alternating pattern for the glazing style of the windows and doors.*

RIGHT, BELOW *Building a conservatory against a house which is thatched is generally a challenge because the roofing materials are very different, and thatch is generally laid to overhang the eaves, giving little room for a second roof beneath. The choice of dark timber is effective, and the irregular profile of the conservatory roof beneath the thatch and window above works well. A. Bartholomew Limited.*

more as a link between the house and the garden; the terrace outside, sheltered but not shaded by the conservatory, makes an ideal place for relaxing and entertaining in balmy weather.

In building a conservatory, the two most important factors are location and size. The location needs to be considered from two aspects. It must look attractive from the outside – ideally, as if it has been designed and built at the same time as the house – but it must also fit in with the room plan. A conservatory approached through utility rooms, down long corridors, away from the hub of things, is a conservatory that will be little used. The actual location will usually involve a compromise between these two considerations. The conservatory, obviously, must be big enough for the proposed function of the room, but not so big that it dominates the main house.

Conservatories for Ordinary Country Homes

BELOW *A simple lean-to graces the double gable of an ancient farmhouse. The unpretentious greenhouse style is perfect for its country garden setting.*

Older farmhouses and cottages were not designed by architects but simply erected using the local building materials and following local tradition, and then adapted to the changing needs of the occupants. Many smaller dwellings today are used as private houses, but as late as the eighteenth century would have housed animals in one part and the farmer and his family in rooms alongside. Dairies, tool sheds, stables, stores, and other buildings will have come and gone with the changing economics of agriculture. To add a conservatory to such a building, even if it is architecturally important, is quite in the tradition of the ad hoc building style, and merely a further adaptation. In practice, careful thought is needed as to how it can be joined to the house. The earlier changes would, in all probability, have been made

using the same roofing material, albeit of varying pitches, but the glass of a conservatory roof would inevitably look awkward at the same level as slate or thatch.

Farmhouses generally have low eaves, and in order to tuck the roof of a conservatory beneath that of a farmhouse, it will often have to be sited against a gable, where there will be greater clear height; alternatively, giving the conservatory a hipped or ridged roof running down to a box gutter at

the abutment with the farmhouse will make a successful join. The problem is most accentuated on thatched houses. They need special care because of the great visual contrast between the thatch and glass, and the especially low eaves that these houses tend to have. A steep pitch to the glass roof leading up to a ridge with timber decoration designed to balance that at the top of the thatched roof helps considerably.

Country houses vary enormously in scale and proportion, and whether it is added to a small, low-lying cottage or a converted mill, the conservatory must be sympathetic to the building. For the cottage, much smaller windows and doors may suit, perhaps in pairs with tiny panes, rather squarish in proportion, and rising to eaves 2 metres (6 feet 6 inches) or even less in height. For the mill, large, somewhat severe-looking doors, and windows rising to eaves 2.2 to 2.5 metres (7 feet 3 inches to 8 feet 3 inches) would be more appropriate. Colour can also be very important in making the conservatory compatible with the main building. For instance, the woodwork need not be all white or white at all; the roof could be

painted a darker colour, to blend in with that of the adjoining house, or natural oak, next to an oak timber-framed house.

Conservatories for Rectories and Vicarages

At the centre of almost every English village is the house that went with the church, usually very well sited, surrounded by trees, and set in a good-size garden. In the eighteenth and particularly in the nineteenth century, most rectors had good incomes from church property (vicars received only a salary) and could afford to improve old property or build new houses for themselves. Many had conservatories added in Victorian times, and these pretty buildings can be seen in photographs and paintings of the period. But the loss of revenue through twentieth-century reform, and the general decline of the Church of England, found clergymen unable to maintain their houses, and the unfashionable conservatories were the first feature to go, followed by the rectories themselves, sold off to help fill the diocesan coffers, while rectors were re-housed in more convenient modern buildings. An owner of one of these fine

LEFT Hook, Norton, Oxfordshire. The familiar bay end to a conservatory is a particularly English feature, providing a gentle finish to the shape of a glasshouse extending from an existing building. The roof, terminated by a series of triangular facets, is very strong and has an attractive, slightly Gothic appearance, particularly from the inside. In this example the corners are emphasized with carved-timber brackets outside and cast-iron braces inside.

BELOW A conservatory tucked into the corner between the high garden wall and the rather plain side of the house greatly improves this part of the garden of a magnificent eighteenth-century rectory. The use of pairs of doors between mullions decorated with classical pilasters suggests an eighteenth-century orangery.

ABOVE, LEFT *The unusual double-ridged design of this conservatory in the Cotswolds has the style of a country greenhouse, which goes very well with the neat rows of vegetables and beanpoles behind. Designed and built by Marston & Langinger 1986.*

eighteenth- or nineteenth-century houses should certainly consider putting back a conservatory if one was originally present or adding one, if not. The garden very often provides an excellent setting with fine evergreen trees and privacy, although it is generally advisable to site it at the back or side of the house rather than the front, unless cars are never parked there.

On older rectories the building may be

planned four-square, with five bays to the main façade and with a central front door. Care will be needed in siting and proportioning the building, as it will inevitably break the symmetry of the house. Very often the best solution will be to design the conservatory so that it has a somewhat detached appearance, perhaps with a hipped roof, with the back slope running down to the house to give a general impression of the

building being constructed against, rather than growing out of, the house wall. It may even be appropriate to detach the main part of the conservatory by connecting it to the house with a short glazed link.

Victorian rectories, with their asymmetrical plans, offer the perfect location from which a conservatory can extend naturally, their high walls leaving plenty of room below the eaves for a tall conservatory roof.

Many Victorian rectories had projecting gables decorated with lacy fretwork, bargeboards, finials, and other features which can be repeated or echoed in the design of the conservatory. It can be built with either a lantern or decorative gables and have fanlights, ornamental brackets, coloured glass, and ridge decoration without looking out of place. If the house once had a conservatory, it may be possible to obtain, through a

ABOVE *Part of a large garden-room glasshouse by Marston & Langinger flanked at each end by a greenhouse and the hothouse which is visible here. The garden room, which opens onto a pretty terrace, is reached from the main, thatched house by walking between ranks of colourful potted plants.*

RIGHT *So that this
conservatory will impinge as
little as possible on the
architecturally important
Queen Anne house it
adjoins, it is reached by a
short, flat-roofed corridor.
This arrangement, with the
conservatory almost free
standing, gives a sense, when
inside, of being in a pavilion
in the garden rather than in a
part of the house. The
moulded stone plinth that
runs around the house has
been carefully matched on the
base of the conservatory. A
substantial moulded timber
cornice at the eaves and
pilasters on the corners lends
an appropriately classical
appearance.*

BELOW *Design for a
conservatory to be added to
an eighteenth-century
country squire's house. The
conservatory, which opens
onto a terrace and leads from
the morning room, has a
solid classical appearance in
keeping with the decorative
details of the house it adjoins.
Fanlights provide a
decorative frieze for the
design and add height.*

public library or local authority conservation officer, information about how it originally looked to provide a starting point for the new design. On smaller buildings, the original may only have been of a lean-to or simple ridged design. These, if carefully proportioned, look very attractive.

Sometimes the old conservatory will still be standing, necessitating a choice between restoration, leaving the single glazing and,

possibly, an inappropriate floor plan, or replacing it with one that has modern comforts, but may lack the period charm of the original. Generally, if the main framework is sound, restoration will simply be a matter of replacing doors and windows, putting on new fittings, restoring the ventilation opening gear (the local blacksmith or engineers will generally help), and re-laying the floor. But if the main framework has

failed, it is nearly always best to start again with a new structure, although any cast-iron components can be stripped, repainted, and used again. Always try to save the old glass, as new sheet glass will lack the imperfections that give it its charm. Any new glass should be cut from horticultural stock – thin small sheets made from dutch-lights and greenhouses that does not have the perfection of float glass used on all new work.

Conservatories for Historic Houses

Special care is needed with historic houses before making any addition or alteration that will affect the appearance and fabric of the building. Owners of fine old houses who want to add a conservatory should go to an architect or designer experienced in working on period property to plan and design the addition. Good drawings, showing not just the conservatory but how it will look in relation to the house, will not only help get the design right but also assist in obtaining planning and listed-building consent. Local conservation officers may be able to provide names and addresses of people experienced in this type of work. The important criteria are appropriate scale and proportions, the correct architectural style, the right details, mouldings, and other decorations, and suit-

The conservatory added to this ancient Wealden house has been constructed of oak, one of the few timbers which can be left unfinished. With time it will mellow and take on the same silvery appearance of the adjoining older woodwork. Designed and built by Martin Miles.

able materials: old bricks or matching stone-work, painted timber, glass, cast iron, and lead, rather than plastic gutters and glazing and stained timber.

Poolhouses

In a climate where sun and warm weather cannot be relied on, and wind prevents enjoyment of good weather, an indoor swimming-pool is an attractive proposition. It also has the advantage of making the pool cleaner by keeping out leaves, insects, and pests. The best use of the space within a

poolhouse is often made with a conventional rectangular pool. Unless it is only to be used as a plunge pool, the minimum size for swimming is about 3.5 metres (11 feet 6 inches) wide by 9 metres (29 feet 6 inches) long, which requires a building of at least 5 metres (16 feet 6 inches) by 11 metres (36 feet) thus allowing a walkway around the pool. As there is no tradition of such domestic buildings, the usual solution is to adopt the styles of agricultural buildings, such as a barn in the country, or a ballroom extension on grander houses or hotels; because these extensions are very large, extra care should be taken not to make them out of scale with the adjoining house.

A glass poolhouse built either in the style of an eighteenth-century orangery or a nineteenth-century conservatory provides a lighter, less imposing alternative and, with a glass roof and sides, will obscure less of the view. A service building will be needed for the pump and filtration equipment, heating, and perhaps an air-conditioning plant. These buildings can turn out to be very large if they include room for changing, a shower, a lavatory, kitchen, sauna, solarium, and so forth. If built against a wall, these service rooms can often be hidden from view. It is sometimes feasible to build an underground room for the pump, filtration and heating equipment which not only gets it out of sight but is particularly effective for suppressing the background hum created by its operation. The alternative is to construct a small, single-storey pavilion proportioned with a sufficiently pitched roof and decoration to make it an attractive feature of the garden. The style of conservatory used as a poolhouse will depend on the location and the style of the surrounding architecture, but

ABOVE *The combination of a shaped pool with curved roofs works very well, and combined with the grotto creates a dramatic effect, particularly at night. The structure, designed by Francis Machin, is entirely metal.*

LEFT *Design for a large poolhouse, square in plan, to be attached to the outbuildings of a Somerset manor house. The roof is divided into four pavilions at the corners, connected by hipped roofs, and the centre has a higher lantern roof.*

LEFT *Design for a conservatory poolhouse. The main façade has seven pairs of doors, which open onto a large lawn. Above them decorative fanlights create the right proportions for a building of this scale. The pool is connected to the house by a curved glazed link.*

ABOVE *The sides of this poolhouse conservatory are made entirely of pairs of doors, all opening outwards, so that in summer the inside can be kept cool, and the views of the fine garden seen to best advantage.*

there are also one or two special consider-ations when the building encloses a pool. The view from the pool itself needs to be taken into account as well as the view from the higher eye-level of people sitting or standing. The glazing should be as low and near to the ground as is practical to avoid obscuring an attractive garden, with panel-ling at the bottom of the doors and windows. On the other hand, from outside, the pool will present an uninteresting void in the middle of the building, so it is important to decorate the side walls, if they are solid, and the area around the pool in an attractive way with planting, furniture, ornaments, murals, and a good colour scheme.

A high proportion of doors opening onto a paved area outside will ensure maximum use of the poolhouse during good weather and will also help keep it cool. In fact, plenty of ventilation with large opening areas in the roof is essential unless the building is fully air-conditioned. In most cases, water heat-ing, coupled with warm-air heating to keep the air temperature a couple of degrees above that of the water, together with double-glazing using low-emissivity glass, will keep condensation to a minimum. A pool cover, either manually or electrically operated, is immensely useful to conserve heat when the pool is not in use and to minimize condensation.

Glazed structures provide an excellent way of joining the main house with nearby cottages, garages, barns, and other outbuild-ings to grant them a new lease of life, either by giving them a different use or making them more accessible. It is also a way of connecting a new poolhouse, dining room, or garden room while retaining the integrity of the two buildings. A conservatory built for this purpose can be a simple corridor, or, if it is wide enough, can be used as an extra room in its own right. Where the buildings are some way apart and a uniform link would be a rather long, unappealing cor-

ridor, the best solution is to create a central pavilion connected to the buildings on each side with short glazed passages. The conservatory at the centre can be any shape, but the arrangement lends itself particularly well to the construction of a round or octagonal building, perhaps one with the roof line emphasized by a lantern or gables.

IN TOWN

The vast majority of homes in English cities and towns are in Victorian terraced or semi-detached houses. The fronts are elaborately decorated with bay windows, imposing entrances, cornices, patterned brickwork, decorative arches, and stucco work, and nobody would want to add a conservatory to such as façade even if there were room. The backs of Victorian houses tell a different story. Plain, and commonly with an extension of one or more storeys housing kitchens, bathrooms, and lavatories, they represent the social divide of Victorian life. The interior would have been planned vertically, with the grand, high-ceiling rooms at raised-ground or first floor level and the plain, smaller rooms at ground or semi-basement level (below stairs) and at the top of the house (children's and maid's bedrooms). Whether occupied as a single dwel-

ABOVE *A small hipped-roof conservatory, rectangular in plan, measuring 4m × 5.5m (13'0'' × 14'6''). The windows and doors have small panes approximating to those on the sash windows of the 1930s house behind. The addition of fanlights to the design adds height and decoration – curved glazing bars are effective in the frieze of fanlights but would look excessive in the doors and windows as well.*

LEFT *The back of the mews house against which the conservatory is built has been opened up into a full-width dining room with three sets of french windows. Three gables, built into the lean-to roof of the conservatory, correspond with these, and beneath the central gable a large pair of doors open into a paved courtyard garden. The bold effect is emphasized by the dark-green exterior. 8.8m × 3m (28'9'' × 9'8'').*

ling or divided into flats, Victorian houses lend themselves well to the alterations necessary for the way we live now. The biggest change is in the bottom rooms, with the bleak scullery, pantry, and kitchen brightened and made comfortable as befits a kitchen used not just for cooking but for family meals. If an L-shaped room is not big enough, it can be enlarged by filling in the gap between the party wall with the neighbours and the rear extension. Building a conservatory provides the maximum natural light to the kitchen behind and a light, decorative contrast to the austerity of the back of the house.

If the roof and sides are double-glazed with high-insulating glass, it is quite practical to use the conservatory all year round as an extension of the kitchen and to open up the wall between the two rooms to create one large and light space. Filling in the space between two walls with a single screen of windows and doors and a lean-to or ridge

ABOVE *Many nineteenth-century terraces were dug into the ground between a sunken back garden and artificially raised street at the front. This enabled the principal rooms to be raised a little, and a kitchen, wash house, utility room, and parlour were set beneath. Constructing a conservatory in the sunken area at the back is an effective way of adapting such houses to modern use.*

OPPOSITE *The conservatory is built on a platform at the end of the house to make the most of the views across south London to the countryside beyond. Underneath the platform the owners have constructed a grotto. Although it has a simple rectangular plan, the conservatory is enriched by carved gutter brackets and a decorative lantern at the apex of the roof.*

57

roof can be very simple. When planning such a conservatory, bear in mind that the view needs to be attractive; otherwise, curtains or blinds will be needed. Constructing a terrace at the same time as the conservatory allows evergreens in strategically placed tubs to obscure unsightly aspects of the view.

In city centres, where space is at a premium, the only available location for a conservatory may be within four existing walls. A hipped roof and box gutters around the perimeter transform a little-used or redundant yard into a very useful and special room, while maintaining a reasonable amount of light through the existing windows covered by the conservatory roof. Ventilation will be needed for the conservatory and for any rooms it covers, but this can be simply achieved by fitting ventilators at the ridge of the new glazed roof.

Rooftop Conservatories

If on the other hand, the view is wonderful, a flat area on the roof, or over a rear extension, makes an ideal location for a conservatory in

BELOW *This prettily glazed conservatory transforms the flat-roofed extension on which it is built and affords a magnificent view of the gardens.*

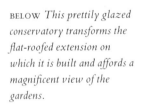

which to sit and watch the sun go down and the night skyline appear. But blinds, obscure glass, or even net curtains may be needed, as everybody around will also be able to look up and see into the conservatory, unless the site is hidden high up on a flat area between pitched roofs and chimneys. A rooftop site makes an excellent conservatory or private

ABOVE *Constructing the conservatory on top of a brick extension to house a new kitchen makes the most of the space at the back of a tall London terrace house. The conservatory leads off the drawing room and gives access to the garden via a timber staircase.*

LEFT *The space beneath this urban flat roof has been transformed by the addition of a decorative 4 metre (13 foot) square roof lantern, and in daytime is a sunny room with large, thriving plants. The roof lantern visible in the background covers a school gymnasium.*

RIGHT *The existing balcony of an end-of-terrace stucco house has been converted into a conservatory with a gracefully curved lead-covered timber roof and subtly proportioned windows. Though small, the addition transforms the room behind, lightening it considerably, and providing a place to sit amongst the plants.*

RIGHT *Sevenoaks, Kent. This modern conservatory has been built in the style of a lean-to vinery typical of the pre-First World War period when this Queen Anne style house was built. Although the doors and windows are single-glazed, the roof is double-glazed with toughened glass, and electric ventilators span the full width at the ridge. Inside, the existing brickwork has simply been clear-sealed and is complemented by a black and red terracotta floor.*

BELOW *Proposal for a first-floor conservatory. Apart from creating additional living space, the conservatory masks the flat roof of a 1920s addition to the beautiful eighteenth-century house. To avoid excessive height, while maintaining a reasonably steep pitch, the top of the roof is flat, with a lead covering.*

sitting room, and, if it is built onto a rear extension, may be entered from the existing staircase, where a pair of prettily glazed doors can brighten the stairwell and provide a glimpse of the conservatory beyond.

Suburban Conservatories

The Victorian conservatory could have been invented to be added to suburban houses with their asymmetrical ground plans, projections and gables, and large leafy gardens which provide the perfect setting. Many of

these houses, built in the first half of the century, have a very attractive, well-planted garden and generous well-planned rooms but small windows and relatively dark interiors. For such a house, a conservatory provides a light and airy room that also extends into the garden and makes the most of the setting. Built out from a rear sitting or dining room, kitchen, or even the hallway, it is very easy to arrange in a satisfactory position in relation to the back of the house, set so that the ridge fits between first-floor windows and without obscuring their view excessively. It is important to bear in mind

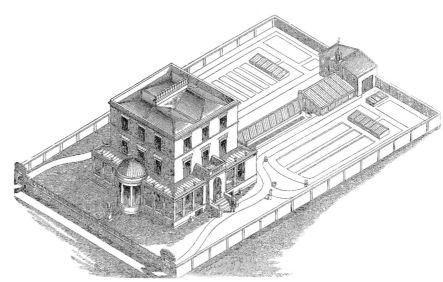

ABOVE *The wrap-around or 'Domicale' conservatory at Mr and Mrs Loudon's home in Porchester Terrace, London, from an illustration in Mrs J. W. Loudon's* The Villa Gardener, *1850. The Loudons were astonishingly energetic, exemplary Victorians. Apart from establishing a large and successful nursery, they wrote and lectured extensively on gardening, landscape design, architecture, furniture, farming, and much more.*

LEFT AND BELOW *Two conservatories, one on the side and one on the back of houses built in city suburbs.*

the orientation of the house and the conservatory and the time of day the sun will strike through the roof and windows. If the conservatory faces east it makes an ideal breakfast room, while if it faces west it will be more suited for late-afternoon and early-evening entertaining.

It is quite feasible to use glass-roofed buildings in all sorts of ways not usually associated with the idea of a conservatory. With suitable shading they make attractive and unusual studies and offices, and can brighten the routine of paperwork although, unless internal partitions are erected, some solid walls will be essential for

ABOVE *Design for a villa in the Italianate style by Gough & Roumieu, an interesting though not entirely successful interpretation of the style in timber and glass.*

RIGHT *An extraordinarily elaborate porch forms the focus of this timber Edwardian conservatory. The designer clearly did not bother to relate the style of the conservatory to that of the rather plainer house with its mellow brickwork and sash windows glazed with margin panes. The change in level between the house and garden has been overcome by sloping the grass up to the base of the conservatory and incorporating some curious stone panels.*

notice boards, shelving, and filing cabinets. If the conservatory is used as a studio, with central worktables, the glass roof, again suitably shaded, will provide the perfect natural illumination. The same is true of a kitchen, but here work surfaces, cooking equipment, and other fittings clustered together in a central group make an effective layout, while a glass lantern with openable fanlights, in the centre of the conservatory roof will cope with kitchen smells and steam and keep the room cool.

SMALL CONSERVATORIES

Not everybody has the space, the right location, or the proper style of house for a large conservatory (a fact which, sadly, does not prevent many people from building one). But if the house will logically support only a small glasshouse, it would be a mistake to regard 'small' as 'inferior'. Though it will not be possible to create a grand, formal room, it will, on the other

Half of this conservatory is used as an artist's studio. The bay end has been closed off with a screen of folding doors to house a collection of plants. The conservatory is sunk into the garden of a city house, and opens onto a small paved area. Designed by Christopher Smallwood and built by Marston & Langinger.

Conservatories at the back of Launceston Place, London, a row of pretty Regency villas. The conservatory in the foreground is decorated with fretwork to match the style of similar porches in the area. The solid lead-covered roof is appropriate for a room used as an office.

baskets to make good use of the space. A big opening in the wall it is built against, so that it extends without any intervening doors from the sitting room, enables it to be used as a large bay window, perhaps with a window seat. The small size will provide an opportunity for decorative patterns of glazing and other ornament, which might be overbearing and too repetitive on a larger scale.

Town or city houses provide many small locations for conservatories, tempting especially because space here will be so much more precious than in the suburbs or in the country. On the front or side of a house, the balcony over a bay window or portico makes an excellent base for a conservatory. Although it may be very small, it can be prettily decorated and furnished, and can be one of the best rooms in an apartment. But because of the size it is best to use it simply, for one purpose: a study, or private office, particularly if it is shady; a quiet sitting room for reading or enjoying the view; an indoor garden, which can be especially valuable for the gardener who must live in a flat. Bear in mind the general rule that the higher the addition, unless it cannot be seen from the street, the harder it is to obtain local authority consent. It may also be necessary to take expert advice on the ability of the structure beneath to support its weight.

Small conservatories were particularly popular in Edwardian times for use as porches, often elaborately decorated with coloured leaded glasswork, and nowhere more so than in seaside resorts where such houses names as 'Seaview' or 'Holmleigh' were often worked into the gable glazing. On a house that lacks an entrance hall they can be very useful for keeping out draughts and storing outdoor clothes as well as housing an armchair that can be turned to the

hand, be easy to achieve a cosy, charming effect impossible in a more spacious conservatory.

An owner of a picture-book country cottage, with thick walls, overhanging eaves, and tiny windows, will appreciate a conservatory which, though small, is bright and affords a panoramic view of the garden. It may only be two or three metres wide, but can make a cosy and pretty addition, furnished with a table and chairs and hanging

path of the sun. With the right design, a porch in the form of a conservatory can add a great deal of character to a plain façade. In America the pleasures and advantages of the veranda are already well known. During the heat of summer it will provide welcome shade from the glaring sun, without necessitating retiring from the garden into the house behind shutters for escape. It is a relatively easy matter to benefit from the light airy space of the veranda throughout the seasons by glazing in a portion of it to make a conservatory. Flyscreens, fans, and blinds can be added as necessary for maximum comfort.

A small conservatory on the terrace of a turn-of-the-century house in Eindhoven, Holland. The sides are double-glazed with single panes of toughened glass in a moulded timber frame screwed to the inside of each panel.

3

SETTING THE SCENE

LANDSCAPING, TERRACING
AND ORNAMENT

OPPOSITE *View of the terrace from one of a pair of glasshouses at Gunton Park designed by Samuel Wyatt (1781–2) as small pavilions at each end of a colonnade. The west one now forms part of a splendid kitchen, while the other houses ancient camellias, in flower here in February.*

The two greatest conservatories in England, the Great Palm House at Kew and the conservatory at Syon House, are set in thoughtfully landscaped gardens with formal arrangements of paths, parterres, statuary, planting, and careful terracing. They both may be seen reflected in water, with a round pool aligned on the central pavilion at Syon House, and a lake the full width of the house at Kew. At Syon there is a central dome with two outer pavilions linked by curved colonnades that enclose the garden in an oval. The buildings are raised a little and open onto a terrace decorated with carved urns, with several steps leading down into a garden with formal beds and lawns divided by gravel paths, and dotted with low, conically clipped trees. Beyond is the pool, with trees behind it. At Kew the Palm House is viewed across a lake behind a terrace built at two levels, with hedges, benches, urns, and grotesque statuary, and the curved glass-and-steel structure is reflected in the water like a huge, shimmering moulded jelly. As at Syon, the landscaping and architecture have been carefully planned to coordinate with the conservatory, and the visual impact is greatly enhanced by the surrounding gardens.

The same will be true of any small domestic conservatory. A well-laid-out terrace and garden around a new building can make all the difference between architectural success and failure. There are three aspects to this: the creation of an attractive, harmonious view from the interior (remember that conservatories are like giant picture windows); the positioning of doors, terracing, and outside steps to make not just a visual but a practical link between the conservatory and the garden; and the integration of the new building into the plan of the garden, house, walls, and other adjacent buildings.

RIGHT *The Morris
Arboretum, near
Philadelphia, privately
owned, is a rare example of
Victorian landscaping which
has survived to the present
day. The conservatory, a
little dilapidated, houses a
rustic bridge, a jungle of tree
ferns, cycads, and smaller
ferns amidst boulders that
create a fantasy of a ferny dell
beneath glass.*

OPPOSITE *The informal
appearance of this lush
garden, surrounding a modest
conservatory built onto a
Victorian London terrace,
has been skilfully contrived
by the garden designer Susan
Gernaey. The York stone
terrace has been entirely
covered, save for a winding
path, with potted plants and
stone ornament, and the
division between the inside
and outside of the
conservatory is blurred by the
free growth of plants.*

INTEGRATION
WITH THE GARDEN

It is important also to bear in mind the style of the garden. If the garden is densely planted and naturalistic, with winding paths disappearing behind trees and shrubs, it may be preferable to blur the transition from conservatory to garden with climbing roses and plants in pots, tubs, or troughs, and beds tight against the base walls, complemented by lots of plants inside. For this garden it may be best to have the doors of the conservatory to one side, leading onto a small paved area, just big enough for a table and chairs, set amongst scented climbers. On the other hand, if the garden is formal, central doors flanked with urns, leading onto a terrace with balustrades and steps, will be more appropriate. The urns, cast-iron or stone, can, as in Victorian gardens, be planted with spiky, architectural plants – agaves, cordylines, or yuccas. In a formal garden, where there is likely to be considerably more paving, and brick or stonework, a conservatory with glass to the ground,

ABOVE *The owners of this beautiful walled garden asked Marston & Langinger to design a working greenhouse. Their solution was a quarter-round design tucked into the corner to use the existing walls on two sides, although these had to be raised to accommodate the apex of the roof. Although the building is decorated with shaped gutters, carved-timber brackets, and pilasters, the general design is deliberately utilitarian, with doors and windows having only vertical bars to divide them.*

rather than low base walls, may be better. Glazing will contrast with the masonry and suggest classical architecture.

Informal Gardens

In the naturalistic garden the conservatory would ideally be set low and enclosed in foliage; in the formal garden, it would be high, with steps leading down to lawns, shrubs, and borders with the levels representing the order of importance of the elements in the scheme. In practice, there may be little opportunity to adjust the level of the conservatory floor in relation to the house and garden outside but it is necessary to start by deciding whether or not there is to be a step into the conservatory from the house, and, if so, whether it is up or down. Using the same floor level as an adjoining room will emphasize that the conservatory is part of the house rather than the garden, and is better if the space is used more as a family room than a place to keep plants. It is rarely appropriate to step up into the conservatory unless the house is set low on a sloping site.

The Sun-trap

If the location is sunny, and the doors lead out to a terrace that is used for relaxing and entertaining, there should be no change in level to the exterior so that the doors can be folded back in warm weather to reveal a continuous floor running out from the conservatory across the terrace. This also makes it easier to carry trays of food and drink to and fro. With such an arrangement it is necessary to have a small break, with a metal water-bar, under the doors to prevent water running into the interior, and a drain outside, in the form of a gully placed beneath the level of the paving, running

LEFT *By aligning the openings and keeping all the levels consistent the five areas shown here are linked in a visual and practical way. The conservatory, square in plan, opens on opposite sides to a paved terrace in the foreground, and a gravelled courtyard behind. To the rear of the courtyard is a study, and behind the Gothic-style chair and desk is a window with a glimpse of the garden beyond. Designed by Stuart Taylor, of Casson Condor & Partners, and Anthony Paine.*

LEFT *Ramshackle sheds were demolished to make way for the conservatory, which serves as an entrance to the house (the door is out of view on the left), a porch-cum-breakfast-room affording a view of a newly created garden – just four years old here. The gable adds height and depth that leaves the view from the two first-floor windows intact.*

This substantial, tall conservatory in Sittingbourne, Kent, is reached from the drawing room through french windows. These are aligned with the conservatory doors, which in turn lead onto a terrace with steps down to the lawn. The building has been double-glazed with low-emissivity glass so that, despite its volume, it is practical to keep warm enough to sit in, even in mid-winter.

along the threshold. This may be covered with either a cast-iron grating or with flagstones, set with a small gap between them to allow water to escape downwards.

Gardens on a Slope

Where a house and garden are built on a slope, there will necessarily be a fall from the conservatory down into the garden below, which can make the conservatory very imposing. It will also increase the likelihood of the room being visible from some way off, so extra-careful planning of the land-scaping will be necessary. If the ground slopes steeply up to the building, care must be taken to avoid the room looking too monumental, unless the house and grounds can support a conservatory in the grand manner. If the banks are sown with grass,

bear in mind that this will not thrive if the ground is too steep, and, in any case, will be difficult to mow – small shrubby plants of an alpine kind are better. Considerable earth movement may be necessary to build out a level platform for both the base and a paved area outside for the doors to open onto, and this can be very expensive, often costing as much, with steps and other work, as the building itself, although the results may be impressive. The floor can be built on joists if the foundations need to go down some way to firm ground, and the space beneath used as a garden store or wine cellar, reached by an outside door, or, if the conservatory is large, by a spiral staircase descending through the floor. Indeed, if there are other rooms at this level, it makes an exciting way of entering the conservatory. With a formal garden, the steps leading down to lawn and

This example shows how, with the right planning and design, the back of a typical nineteenth-century London house can be improved with the addition of a conservatory. It spans the full width of, and is linked with, the kitchen and drawing room.

beds, and the balustrading and piers, constructed of stone, cast stone, or (if you live in a town) cast-iron, which gives a lighter effect, can be an important feature. Alternatively, in a more informal garden, banks should be constructed so that they rise gently, with a path winding upwards with steps cut in at intervals. The path will be less imposing if it is built at the side, perhaps against the house.

The Sunken Conservatory

If the conservatory floor level must be below that of the garden, as is so often the case with nineteenth-century houses, a courtyard will be needed outside the conservatory to allow the doors, if they open outwards, to swing back, and to provide space at the bottom of the steps up into the garden. Waterproofed retaining walls will be needed for the base of the building where it is cut into the garden, and the windowsills must be at least 150 millimetres (6 inches) – 225 millimetres (9 inches) is better – above the ground level outside. This arrangement, with the conservatory sunken, can create a cosy, insulated feeling inside but it is important to

limit the choice of plants surrounding the conservatory to those that will be low enough not to obstruct the windows. Paving or a path running around the perimeter will help keep growth back from the glass, and reduces the risk of damp. If the basement area is greater than that of the conservatory, do not have a narrow walkway around the exterior, as this can be unattractive, and creates a dead area. If it is unavoidable, a base of timber panelling will give a lighter, brighter aspect to the exterior than one of masonry, and a bank planted out with a range of interesting plants can be substituted for the usual brick retaining walls.

PLANTS, PATHS AND PAVING

On an old house, the new walls forming the base of the conservatory, particularly if they are brick, will take a few years to weather down and match the older work. If narrow beds are built at the base, plants can be grown to mask the new walls. Choose varieties, preferably evergreen, which will not grow too high and interfere with the opening of the windows; lavender, dwarf

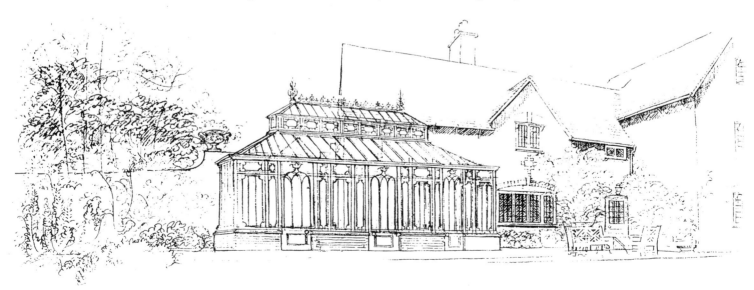

varieties of rosemary, and box, for instance, are suitable. The shape of the building can be emphasized by a path running around the outside, widening into a terrace at the doorways. There are numerous paving materials, including concrete imitations of natural materials, some of which are very good; in the long run, though, nothing is as good as the real thing. Natural stone flags roughly dressed into squares or rectangles of assorted sizes, randomly laid, will work well for most people; the joints can be filled with a mixture of sharp sand and garden soil,

LEFT *A carefully planned mixture of old and new. The plainness of new brick is avoided by the panels of randomly coursed stone, constructed in the local tradition, with tiny stones pressed into the pointing, once used to strengthen the mortar. The windows are double-glazed in the old way with pairs of matching hinged casements that open in and out.*

from which small plants can be coaxed into growing. Brick is attractive, but do make sure to use proper frost-proof paving rather than house bricks. These can be laid in staggered courses herringbone fashion or mixed with flints, small stone flags, or granite sets. Cobbles (small round beach pebbles) are suitable only for paths that are not much used (they are not very comfortable to walk on), but can be inexpensively laid in beautiful patterns by picking different shapes and colours – something popular a hundred years or more ago. Granite sets make excellent slip-resistant paving and usually come in 10- to 15-centimetre (4- to 6-inch) cubes. They can also be used decoratively for the edges of paths, level or raised a little, and perhaps set at an angle, to define

the boundary. A charming alternative, a Victorian revival, are salt-glazed terracotta tiles cast into rope and other patterns, set vertically around the perimeter of paved areas and paths.

Many people use their conservatories in much the same way as a paved terrace. The conservatory is a family room for relaxing on wicker loungers or sofas, pottering amongst the plants, or having informal meals. This is also very much how the terrace might be used in warm weather, so it is logical that the two should be used together, with the conservatory doors opening onto the terrace. If this is what is wanted, it is essential to design the terrace and conservatory together, planning and constructing the conservatory base, terrace, steps, beds and other features as one project. A conservatory has the advantage of providing shelter while scarcely restricting the light, and, if the building projects out from the house, a protected space can be paved that is ideal for a garden table and chairs, a barbecue and growing plants in tubs and

LEFT Conservatory at Wave Hill, in the grounds of an estate garden overlooking the Hudson River in New York City. The building is a curious combination of the old (an eclectic classical entrance porch) and the new (a metal framed glasshouse with curved eaves). A path outside leads down to a circular paved terrace, with attractive, clipped, pot-grown plants.

LEFT The perfect conservatory for this Victorian Gothic cottage. The conservatory gables, with their lacy bargeboards and the narrow, arched-topped windows, and doors, faithfully follow the style of the house.

RIGHT *A page of ornamental urns from* The Villa Gardener *(1850), which seems to have been written for the head gardeners or owners of houses on the scale of Versailles. Urns such as these are easily obtainable in reproduction cast iron, terracotta, or reconstituted stone.*

BELOW *A conservatory on a Victorian Gothic house with beds right up against the base of the structure and a pair of urns to either side of the double doors. Note the change in level.*

pots, especially those that need shielding from the wind.

GARDEN ORNAMENT

The paths and terracing outside the building may be decorated, and the steps and doorways emphasized, by urns or statuary standing directly on the paving or set on pedestals. There are numerous reproduction cast-iron patterns, indistinguishable from the originals, and these can either be left to rust, which does them no harm, or painted in dark colours, such as bottle green, chocolate brown, red oxide (which is very attractive), or paler shades, such as grey-green or buff. Do not paint them white – the effect will be harsh and inappropriate. When planting cast-iron urns, bear in mind that metal is a good conductor of heat. The plants inside them must be able to withstand high temperatures and risk drying out in summer – agaves are ideal. Antique stone urns, vases, and statuary are much in demand and consequently expensive, although cast-stone imitations are often of a high standard and mellow with time and the growth of moss

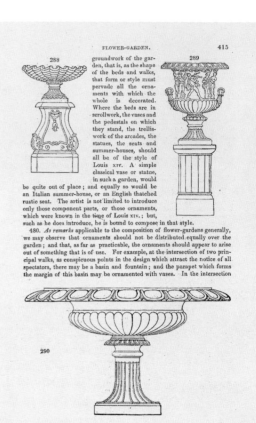

and lichen. These items are also made of terracotta and traditional salt glaze, usually a deep brown or bluish colour, with a sheen.

Saving Rainwater

In a hard-water district the glass roof can be drained into a cistern to provide soft rainwater for watering conservatory and pot plants, particularly if they are not lime-tolerant. Oak butts are still made and sold secondhand by coopers, who will also supply traditional turned wooden taps for them. Stand them on bricks, paint the hoops to stop them rusting, and brush the staves with creosote or oil and they will last for many years. It should be remembered that they are not watertight until after they have been filled for a day or so and the wood has expanded; if the water level drops too low,

they will leak. A more expensive, beautiful alternative is a lead tank, either an antique one, decorated with seventeenth- or eighteenth-century patterns (and usually the date), or one of the excellent reproductions cast from old designs. A lid should be constructed, ideally of oak, to keep the leaves out. It is usual to float a small quantity of paraffin on the surface (it does not taint the water) to prevent mosquitoes breeding. An overflow should be provided, leading into a drain.

This conservatory at Hampton, Middlesex, is built on top of a garage converted into a kitchen. It is used as a dining room reached from below by a spiral staircase and dumbwaiter.

PART II

THE
CONSERVATORY
FROM THE
INSIDE

4

LIVING UNDER GLASS

DIVERSE USES, APPROACHES, AND DECORATIVE EFFECTS

Glass buildings, with their bold architectural quality created by high roofs and exposed structural features, provide an exciting opportunity for interior decoration in styles not possible elsewhere in the house. Success will depend on making the structure as decorative as possible, having a clear vision of how the room is to be used, and choosing the right colours, furnishings, and fittings. Housing a collection of plants will, for some, be of first importance, in which case the arrangement of the interior will depend very much on their cultural requirements. For others they will be a backdrop for furniture and ornaments, with the selection and position of plants designed to suit the overall furnishing plan. But even in the conservatory devoted to plants, fashion and personal taste will have a strong effect on the style of the interior.

GENERAL CONSIDERATIONS

The interior needs to be considered at the earliest stages of planning; the building's size, location, and orientation all have a bearing on the inside. It is essential from the beginning to resolve the purpose of the building and the way the space will be used, and to give thought to the general style and the way the internal furnishings and furniture will be arranged. A clear vision of these aspects of the building is important in determining size, the number and position of doors, and the type of decorative features, such as the pattern of glazing bars, the plainness or richness of mouldings, and the extent to which decorative metalwork is employed. One of the commonest problems preventing the effective use of a conservatory is having too many doors, or having them in an awkward place, leaving little scope for arranging the furniture in a comfortable and logical manner. Another frequent problem is a lack of walls on which to

A large conservatory designed and built by Marston & Langinger to provide a comfortable, well-lit garden room leading off the rather dark library it adjoins. The floor, close-covered with seagrass matting, has white cast-iron grilles covering underfloor heating set beneath the specially made window seats. The building is shaded by a combination of three materials: Colefax & Fowler curtains, Holland blinds over the windows, and pinoleum blinds in the roof.

PREVIOUS PAGES *Web of wrought iron and miniature glass panes that make up the dramatic dome of the Palm House at Bicton.*

A garden studio designed by architect Anthony Collett for his own house. The roof, made of twelve square glass panels, is supported on Douglas fir columns. The eaves of the roof have matchboarding painted dark green to contrast with the varnished rafters. Much use has been made of forged ironwork – straps, brackets, hinges, and bolts, as well as the large central lamp.

OPPOSITE *The conservatory of floral decorator Ken Turner is mainly used as a dining room. It is painted and furnished in sombre dark greens and blues and decorated with seasonal floral arrangements.*

hang mirrors or place furniture with backs not designed to be seen. Building a conservatory into a corner, using existing walls, can help solve this. A further important consideration when planning the building is the view: the thought of bare walls, unattractive outbuildings, parked cars, or neighbours (especially if you are not on good terms!) can prevent enjoyment of the room, although an intricate pattern of glazing bars, carefully trained climbers, blinds, patterned or coloured glass, or even curtains may help obscure the outlook.

The texture and finish of the materials used in the construction and furnishing of the conservatory are vital ingredients in determining the way it will look. For example, the building may be glazed with large, undivided panes set in a metal framework and have a polished marble floor and tabletops and glossy-leaved plants. Or it might have small panes set in natural timber,

or matt-painted frames, walls of crumbly brick or stone (or plastered, with a textured finish), a floor of rough stone or country terracotta tiles, antique furniture with a patina of rust or verdigris, and plants with finely divided leaves and irregular growth. It should be borne in mind that these two rooms will have markedly different acoustic properties. The first will create sharp, echoey sounds reflecting off the smooth surfaces; the second, with more absorbent surfaces, will muffle sound. Even the division of glazing into large or small panes has a considerable effect.

The framework of most conservatories is painted white, which can be a harsh contrast to the adjoining walls and woodwork and certainly does not go with the foliage of the plants within. Its use derives from the practice of painting the woodwork of old horticultural buildings with cheap, long-wearing white lead. Colour has no effect on the price or durability of modern paint. The exterior must be finished to complement the colours of the surrounding buildings, usually with soft, muted hues, perhaps warm off-white or cream, buff or stone colour, providing a lighter range, grey-greens, grey-blues and khakis in the middle, and dark green, or if you are in a city, dark blue, or even red if a deep colour is required. It is worth noting that, while the exterior colour will not be visible inside, the interior paintwork can be seen from the outside, so, if you are using different colours, you must consider how they will look together. Inside, the floor, walls, framework, furniture and plants are all elements of the colour scheme and mood of the room, so a plan must be worked out for these as well. This will help unify the room so that if, for example, red is being used, metalwork and features on the framework can be picked out in red, furnishing fabrics chosen to coordinate with it, and plants selected for the colour of their blossom or foliage (poinsettias in winter, perhaps). Flooring material also needs to be decided on quite early, as the floor will provide the largest expanse of colour in the room. The orientation of the building and the amount of sun it receives will also influence the colour scheme. When choosing colours, take into account that the atmosphere of the room will be quite different at night, and that, unless the blinds are pulled down, the glass will reflect lamps and brightly coloured objects.

CONSERVATORY AS DINING ROOM

Conservatories can make wonderful, stylish dining rooms for eating under the stars, amongst plants, but beneath the warmth and shelter of glass. A daytime table with a slate, marble, or glass top can be covered for evening with a cloth and laid with candlesticks or hurricane lamps so that the meal can be lit by candlelight reflected in the glass roof. Floral china is particularly appropriate in this setting, and the table can be decorated with plants in pots (cut flowers never seem quite right in a conservatory). Mirrors – perhaps with gilt or painted frames – can increase the feeling of space and amount of reflected light. If a lamp is to be hung over the table, you need to find a logical position in the roof for it. Lanterns or chandeliers may be used, but, if the latter, avoid one that has elaborate cut-glass decoration.

As with any dining room, the conservatory dining room is best located as near the kitchen as possible. This is often done by opening up the kitchen wall and building on

ABOVE *The highly stylized interior of a rooftop conservatory built as a dining room with views across the treetops of Kensington. The woodwork is painted a bright rust red inside and out, and matching barley-twist columns decorate the framework. As the conservatory faces north, and there are few plants to create a humid atmosphere, it is possible to have a polished timber table, although not a valuable one which would fade in the light. This example is painted and grained in imitation of walnut.*

LEFT *The dramatic appearance of the roof of this Surrey conservatory (Marston & Langinger, 1988) is created by the crucifix plan and a steep pitch, with three gables to the outside and one connected to the gable of the house behind.*

ABOVE *An old conservatory built to house vines and rows of pots on staging has been cleaned, repaired, and repainted for use as an informal day-room adjoining the formal interior of an eighteenth-century mansion. The old cast-iron and stone staging survives in the conservatory, as does the maker's name cast into the ironwork of the roof.*

87

ABOVE, LEFT *Although it is
constructed of aluminium,
this conservatory, with its
lacework of painted castings,
has an authentic nineteenth-
century apearance. The soft
verdigris colour is very
successful and blends in with
the greens of the oaks and
landscape that surround the
conservatory. It is
illuminated inside by tiny
low-voltage lamps painted to
match – there is one visible at
the foot of the balustrade.*

a conservatory to create a double room, with kitchen fittings and a table at one end and dining chairs and table, perhaps set amongst some fine plants, at the other, close enough to make serving easy but far enough away to keep food preparation and clutter out of sight. As kitchens are usually built on the north side of a house to keep them cool in summer, it is unlikely that a conservatory dining room will get much direct sun.

CONSERVATORY AS KITCHEN

In a spot well shaded from the sun, there is no reason why the kitchen itself cannot be built under glass, especially as it will then receive plenty of light and ventilation. Un-less the oven, hobs, sink and work surfaces are clustered together in a central group, at least one wall of the building will need to be solid, to support a tall refrigerator or fridge-freezer and eye-level wall cabinets. A simple lean-to design can be very effective, with the cooking area along the rear solid wall so that steam and cooking smells can escape through ventilators at the ridge, and sink and washing equipment along the outside wall. The latter should be designed with masonry walls 900 millimetres (3 feet) high, to mask the fittings from the exterior and with windows above the glass starting just above worktop level, giving plenty of light to work by and a view from the sink. It is essential to use double-glazing in a kitchen, not just to retain heat but to minimize

LEFT *The richly coloured interior of conservatory builder Alexander Bartholomew's home.*

BELOW *This kitchen's original window was replaced by a wider opening* *reaching almost to the ceiling so that the conservatory functions very effectively as a breakfast room. The floors of the conservatory and the kitchen are on the same level and covered with the same hand-made terracotta tiles.*

LEFT *The existing kitchen was modified and extended with a conservatory which has a complementary style.*

BELOW *A skylight, built like a miniature conservatory over an opening in a flat roof, can provide natural light and ventilation over a studio, kitchen or garden room.*

ABOVE *A timber-and-metal conservatory furnished in pastel colours. The terracotta floor leads out to a terrace on the same level and gives a greater sense of the garden indoors. Around the walls narrow staging is supported on delicately turned timber columns.*

The conservatory spans the walled garden of a London terrace house to create a huge, brightly lit additional living room for a garden flat. The doors fold back on themselves to make a broad opening. A subtle, soft-green paint was chosen for a gentle transition from house to garden.

condensation, worse here than in any other room in the house apart from the bathroom. Ordinary conservatory roller blinds for the roof and side windows are ideal, and, if the conservatory is constructed of timber, there will be plenty of places to fix hooks, rails, lamps, and kitchen equipment. Shelves can generally be fitted, perhaps on decorative metal brackets, at eye level across the windows, and if these are divided into small panes, positioned to align with the horizontal glazing bars.

CONSERVATORY AS FAMILY ROOM

A family room is by far the most common use made of conservatories. They are ideal for relaxing in with the children, for chatting when the neighbours drop by, for having breakfast and reading the Sunday newspapers, and for providing a spot for the

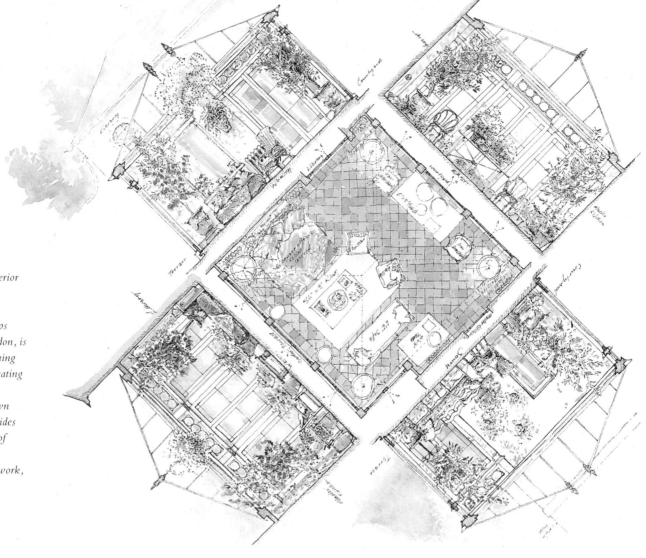

RIGHT *Design for a conservatory and its interior decoration by Anthony Paine, 1986. The conservatory for an 1830s villa in Highgate, London, is used for casual entertaining with various kinds of seating and a table for informal dining. This folded-down elevation drawing provides the most complete idea of how the room and its decorative scheme will work, both functionally and aesthetically.*

OPPOSITE *A conservatory decorated for Christmas. A conservatory provides plenty of scope for fairy lights, paper decorations, baubles, and such Christmas flowers as red poinsettias,* Amaryllis hippeastrum, *and other bulbs brought on early. The walls can be decorated with swags of evergreens – laurels, yew, and holly – trimmed with walnuts and small round oranges.*

cat to bask in the sun. The rugged floors, and furniture, free from polished surfaces, used in most conservatories are ideal for children: if something is spilt, no harm is done. The glass roof and sides provide plenty of light for reading, writing, sewing, household repairs, or sketching, and so the conservatory becomes a natural centre for leisure activities. With this in mind, plan a space big enough for a table that will take four or more chairs, a side table, a wicker or old upholstered sofa, an armchair or two, perhaps a lounger and footstool, room for

plants in pots, ornaments, stereo speakers, and all the paraphernalia of everyday living. Choose warm colours for the room and cheerful fabrics for cushions and tablecloths. An old rug or kilim will brighten and soften an open area on the floor, or give a cosy look in front of sofas or armchairs. Pick plants which are easy to grow and have a long flowering season; as the room is primarily for people, it is not practical to attempt serious horticulture in the same space.

A conservatory can make a perfect studio for a designer or painter working at home.

North light with no direct sunlight (which is far too bright to work by effectively) is best. If that is not possible, fit cloth blinds but make sure irritating shafts of sunlight do not shine between them. An internal courtyard covered with a roof of glass makes an effective use of space and creates an ideal studio. In town, a flat area on the roof is a wonderful location for a conservatory studio. With a glass roof there is no need to position worktables under windows, but remember that after dusk plenty of bright lamps will be needed, as a lot of their light will be lost through the glass.

CONSERVATORY AS GARDEN ROOM

If your house is large and the conservatory is not essential for living space, it is likely that it will be used as an occasional garden room, furnished with garden chairs and tables and fine specimen plants. With a separate greenhouse, pots can be brought in when flower buds start opening, and replaced with others as the season progresses, giving the room a different mood with each season, starting with jasmine, camellias, mimosa, spring bulbs, agapanthus, bougainvillea, plumbago through to the summer, followed by autumn bulbs and vallota and finishing with late-flowering chrysanthemums, hyacinths, amaryllis that has been brought forward, and poinsettias for Christmas. Trellises for climbers provide attractive decoration for the walls but have to be specially designed and made. The ordinary garden centre sort is too crude for inside use, but there are a number of specialist firms who produce beautiful patterns based on traditional styles. If the room is large, arrange the furniture in groups which can be modified for different

ABOVE *This simple lean-to makes a comfortable family room. In the foreground is a blue 'cathedral stove'.*

LEFT *A quarter-round conservatory tucked into the corner of an eighteenth-century house. The floor is made of old stone flags saved from the former terrace.*

OPPOSITE *The combination of woodwork, floor, old furniture and faded kelim cushions has created a comfortable, relaxing atmosphere.*

95

occasions; a good-size conservatory used in this way will be excellent for parties, especially for summer ones if the doors open onto a terrace.

It will not be practical to use the conservatory for entertaining if it also houses a collection of plants of any size. Moving them out to make room for a party will be time-consuming, and it will only be possible to put them outside if the weather is right for them. It is feasible to house a plant collection in a room that is also used for people if the varieties chosen require moderate humidity and temperature. There are many plants from temperate regions that will do well in these conditions, but they will need a heating system designed to provide a minimum temperature of, say, 10°C (50°F) throughout

ABOVE *The owners of this conservatory in Pennsylvania use it as a garden room. It has a central glass-topped table and low chairs amid statuary, hanging baskets, and potted cyclamens. At night it is lit with antique storm lanterns.*

LEFT *A confusion of growth in a conservatory which each winter is made over to plants. In spring some of the pots will be moved out and replaced with tables and chairs. In flower here are several varieties of abutilon, cyclamen, streptocarpus, clivia, and plumbago, and in the foreground a thorn apple.*

97

LEFT *In summer the outside doors of this south London conservatory are left permanently open, providing a gentle transition from the garden to the drawing room. In the conservatory grow* Lapageria rosea, *white oleander, tibouchina and the climber tetrastigma.*

OPPOSITE *Nineteenth-century Chinese ceramic seat with a beautiful turquoise glaze. These were imported in quantities in Victorian times, when they were popular for conservatory seating.*

ABOVE *Winter Gardens, Somerleyton Hall, Suffolk. This scene, probably photographed around the time of the First World War, shows the conservatories at the start of their decline still planted in Edwardian fashion with lots of maidenhair and asparagus ferns. The planting directs the eye to an alabaster nude at the centre of the main house. Though richly embellished with architectural decoration, the conservatories here were regarded as superior greenhouses, as shown by the pools of water left lying in the pathway.*

LEFT *An old lean-to conservatory with pretty overlapping Gothic-style glazing bars. The floor is original and is made of Norfolk pamnents, thick terracotta tiles traditionally used in malthouses. In the foreground the violet blossom of* Hardenbergia violacea *can be seen.*

shrubs in containers or borders, and, finally, hanging baskets and climbers in the roof. Avoid deciduous plants where there is furniture and also plants that produce quantities of blossom that might drop onto cushions and tabletops. Lighting amongst the foliage gives a pretty effect, but make sure the plants are kept clear of the fittings. A conservatory furnished in this way has a good traditional style and makes for a very attractive, un-strenuous year-round form of gardening, protected from the weather. The gardener can then sit amongst his specimens studying their growth, appreciating the successes (and the incomparable pleasure of seeing a new plant flower for the first time) and, from the comfort of an armchair, keep a vigilant eye out for disease and pests.

DECORATIVE EFFECTS

Victorian Pastiche

A conservatory built in a Victorian style on a house of that period, may be decorated and furnished in the same period. In this case, the floor should be paved with terracotta tiles in geometric patterns, perhaps with a border or central motif in black, red, buff, and brown. Victorian floors also used smaller amounts of white, green, and bright blue. The heating should be provided by an under-floor system with cast-iron grilles forming a border around the edge, or by squat, cast-iron radiators without covers. The framework should be painted in broken white or combinations of cream, buff, and brown. Ideally, the building should have cast-iron brackets and braces which can be picked out in bright colours using red or green. There should be plenty of plants, including palms and ferns.

the year twenty-four hours a day. The plants should be arranged so that there is foliage and blossom at all levels from the floor to the top of the roof. This can be achieved with small, low shade plants, ferns, mind-your-own-business, selaginellas, pots on the ground containing plants of varying size, staging a little higher, pots on stands, tall

Aspidistras in decorated and glazed pots are very much of the period. Wire and china jardinières planted out with brightly coloured flowers would also have been used. Lots of occasional bamboo and wicker furniture, small cane tables and upholstered chairs, Moorish and Indian lamps, tables inlaid with small pieces of mother-of-pearl (keep those, however, out of direct sunlight), and low tables with engraved brass tray-tops are typical of a Victorian interior. The walls could have decorative trellising, or short shelves on brackets to support pots. The side tables might hold plant containers, either round or in the shape of caskets, fashioned to look as if they were made of twigs or ornamented with shells arranged in patterns. To complete the Victorian floral sitting room, add alabaster statues of draped nudes and a cast-iron or stone fountain with a cherub on top.

The Classical Interior

The cool classical interiors of period orangeries provide an inspiration for the interior decoration of shady conservatories and those with more than one solid side — for example, a courtyard which has been glazed over. These grand and sparsely furnished rooms relied on a bold architectural effect. The floor would have been of stone flags with a natural, honed finish; in later examples, under-floor heating would have been installed in a duct running around the perimeter covered by cast-iron grilles in Greek or Roman decorative patterns. For a more refined effect, the floor design might have been enriched with diagonally set corner keys of slate or black Purbeck marble or, more elaborately, a circular or oval centrepiece of varicoloured marbles. The main

part of the floor was often set at a low level, with one or two steps around the edge supporting columns or pedestals for statuary. Stucco was popular for solid walls painted in earth colours – umber, sienna, and terracotta – while the woodwork would have been in shades of grey or off-white or painted to imitate stone. Furnishings would include wooden console tables, painted or gilded, with marble tops on which urns or Roman busts were placed. The seating

INTERIORS

would consist of stone benches or straight-backed metal chairs; no soft furnishings would have been used in this restrained atmosphere. Palms, tree ferns, oranges, lemons, camellias and other evergreen trees and shrubs in venerable tubs and pots were alternated with the statuary; a particularly grand specimen might have been used at the

OPPOSITE *Dudley House, Park Lane, London, 1890. Many of the attractive verandas with copper- or lead-covered concave roofs that were built onto the backs of Regency houses were, in later years, glassed in to provide conservatories or early 'sun rooms'.*

LEFT *From* Fragments on the Theory & Practice of Landscape Gardening, *H. Repton, 1816. Repton's 'before-and-after' marketing approach was advanced for his day. The illustrations show how a dreary existence can be transformed into a sparkling social life.*

centre of the floor, with the foliage rising to the roof. Lighting would have been provided by candles or hanging lanterns.

This style was adapted in late-nineteenth-century stone and iron and glass buildings as ferneries came into fashion, with more attention paid to planting and less to classical detail. Though much the same as traditional orangeries, they included beds to create small forests of ferns, cycads, and tree ferns, often crossed by winding paths and edged with rocks dripping with small ferns and creepers. These buildings of the 1860s and 1870s were meant to be inhabited by plants rather than people – the only role of the latter was to wander through admiring the exotic foliage.

The cool, peaceful style of these classical eighteenth- and nineteenth-century interiors is particularly suited to modern conservatories which have been created out of a wide corridor or atrium, with a glass roof. Such spaces are generally used to link rooms together, and so would not be used for sitting anyway. When choosing materials for paint, subdued colours are best. The furniture should have a serious, masculine quality. For a very grand effect, the walls could be divided into panels with plaster, or painted timber, pilasters rising to a bold cornice. If the space is large – and, especially, if the roof needs support, one or more aisles of columns can be introduced, between which fine specimen plants may be grown. For a lighter effect, the walls could be painted with *trompe l'œil* murals to give an illusion of open arches with a sylvan landscape beyond.

The Orangery, Kensington Palace, built in 1704. The cool, white interior, illuminated by huge sash windows has carvings by Grinling Gibbons and impressive statuary, thought to be by Francavilla, in the niches.

RIGHT *The Compleat Angler Hotel on the Thames at Marlow, Buckinghamshire. The Regency design of this new conservatory arose from a planning requirement that the height should not exceed that of the earlier, tiled building to the left.*

OPPOSITE RIGHT *Interior of a conservatory designed by Peter H. Slinger R.I.B.A. and built by Alexander Bartholomew Limited. To the left, a timber-and-glass screen provides a space to create a passage from the hotel entrance. The cool, austere style is enhanced by the marble floor tiles.*

OPPOSITE, LEFT *A design adapted by the manufacturers Amdega Limited from their catalogue for the bar of a hotel in Belgium.*

BELOW *In this painting by Hugo Berger, a lively luncheon party of Scandinavian artists takes place in the conservatory attached to a Parisian cafe of about 1880.*

CONSERVATORIES FOR OFFICES, HOTELS AND RESTAURANTS

Glass buildings are increasingly used commercially, for hotel restaurants and lounges and for shops, offices, and studios. As on private houses, they should be architecturally sympathetic with period property, and allow natural light into the rooms they are built over. If used as restaurants, it is essential that they provide a pretty view for the diner. Decorative glasshouses make perfect shops for plant nurseries and are charming for florists. Traditional conservatories are generally regarded as being suitable only for private offices, but with sympathetic architectural detail and interior decoration may be surprisingly appropriate for business use. A floor of polished marble, limestone or granite, terrazzo, or natural linoleum that is plain, marbled, or cut into patterns gives a striking modern look. The walls should be smooth and the furniture of chrome, nickel, leather, and the like, sparsely arranged to create a cool, uncluttered, and orderly mood. Use metal or wooden venetian blinds or plain Holland fabric roller blinds, white opal globes for hanging lamps. Alternatively, fit spotlamps (small or low-voltage ones fitted to the framework of the roof are the least obtrusive) but do not use low-level spots or uplighters – the light will simply be lost through the glass or reflected glaringly back inside. It is important that the humidity be kept to a minimum, so any plants chosen (*Ficus benjamina*, for instance) must thrive in dry conditions. Finally, the heating and ventilation must be thermostatically controllable, to ensure an even temperature.

5

THE IMPORTANCE OF DETAIL

ARCHITECTURAL FEATURES

OPPOSITE *A conservatory provides an opportunity to use pretty architectural features such as these curved glasing bars, which would have been out of place on the adjacent house.*

The structural framework of conservatories lends itself particularly well to embellishment with decorative details, such as columns and pilasters, brackets, cornices, crestings, and finials. Old catalogues of nineteenth- and early-twentieth-century manufacturers reveal this only too well, with their elaborate designs, iced with a confusion of decoration. This was partly a result of the development of mass production in the Industrial Revolution and the consequent introduction of catalogues of ready-made ornament in cast iron and timber. The Scottish company Walter Macfarlane produced a catalogue of two volumes listing thousands of components cast from patterns at their Saracen Foundry in Fossil Park, Glasgow. Both the Victorian and Edwardian conservatories that supported this elaborate decoration were often not particularly well made and finished; waterproofing was poor, and the structural and decorative components were crudely bolted together, with the timber parts merely nailed to create the desired effect, making them extremely difficult to maintain. The simple maxim pronounced with designs of this period in mind – that one should decorate construction, not construct decoration – still holds true; decorative details should form part of the necessary framework and features of the building or emphasize them rather than being tacked on as an afterthought. Gutters can be moulded to form a cornice, or supported on cast brackets, to point up junctions and the divisions between the framework beneath. Mullions can be

RIGHT *Rich decoration built up in painted timber with pilasters rising up to an elaborate cornice, the upper part of which is an extruded metal gutter, shaped to disguise its purpose. The cornice is stopped above the doors to unify them with the portico above.*

BELOW *Just one of more than a hundred pages on railings from Walter Macfarlane & Company's two volume illustrated* Catalogue of Castings, *Saracen Foundry, Glasgow.*

OPPOSITE *Conservatory fittings: enamelled cast metal is ideal for ridge crestings, finials, staging and shelf brackets, as it is durable and easily made into elaborate patterns. The section of moulded-metal gutter has been especially designed for conservatories by Marston & Langinger. A poorly-designed or badly fitted gutter can ruin the external appearance of a conservatory.*

worked with mouldings and have classical details such as surbases and pilasters, which in turn can be decorated, and carved capitals. The roof may be topped with a turned ball or finial of timber or cast iron, and the ridge fitted with cresting of carved wood or metal, cast in lacy patterns, to provide interest to the skyline. Decorative features of the house, such as cornice mouldings, eaves brackets, brickwork and window details can readily be adapted to the scale and proportions of the conservatory.

Unless the design is an exercise in pure modernism, it is essential to relieve the plainness with mouldings. This is most important on the inside. Plain, square glazing bars are used only on greenhouses and other basic, utilitarian buildings. Conservatory glazing bars should be moulded, not only to give them a finished appearance but to reduce their bulk, providing a clearer, less interrupted, view through the glass. Glazing bars gradually decreased in thickness from the time of Queen Anne until, by the middle of the last century, they were often little more than half an inch thick, tapering to a

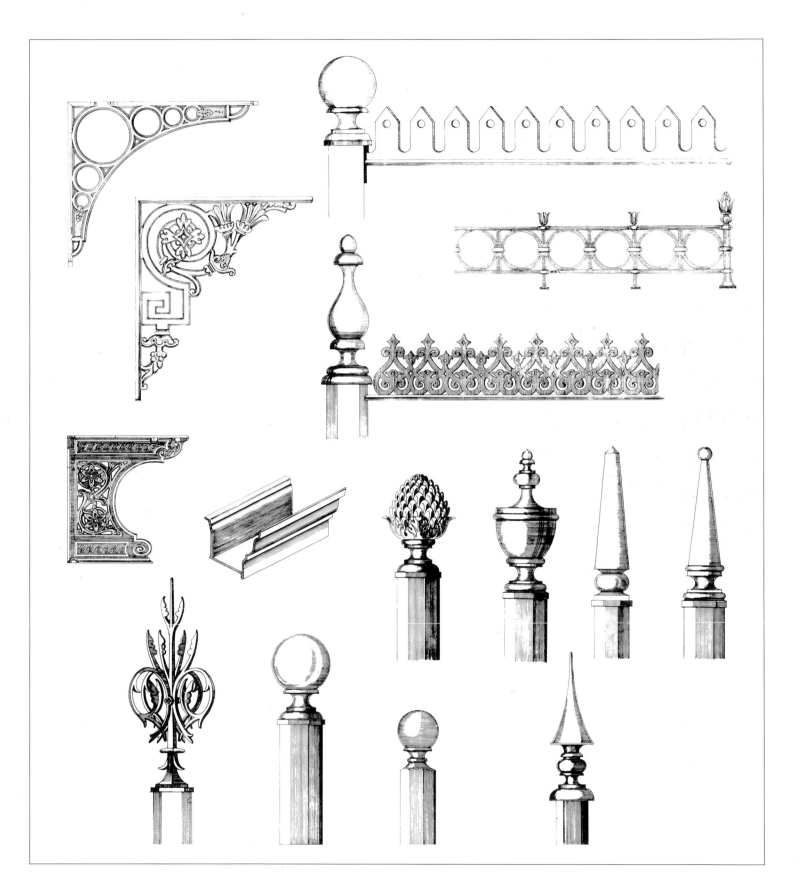

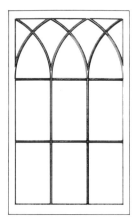
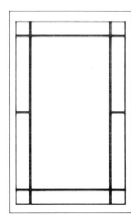
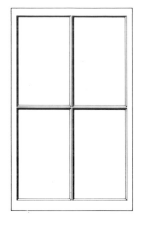
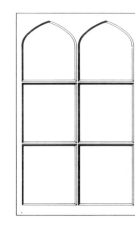
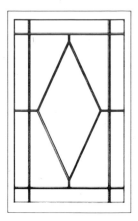

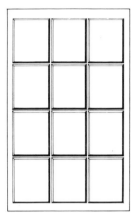
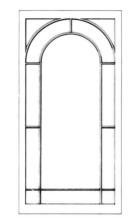
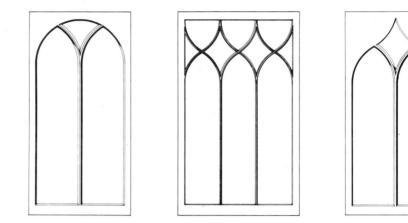

fine inside edge. If the conservatory is to match woodwork on an existing building, this should be taken into account, and the new mouldings conform with the old.

A wide board on the inside of the window sills, moulded at the edge, and running around base walls, provides a useful shelf for plants; it can be made up to 450 millimetres (18 inches) deep, by supporting it with decorative timber or cast-metal brackets. A cornice constructed around the inside of the eaves makes a clear division between walls and roof, creates architectural interest, and can be used to hide the bases of roller blinds or lamps. Cast-iron braces are sometimes fitted at the eaves to stiffen the framework of the roof and these soften the line of the junction and provide a good place to hang baskets. They are occasionally fitted at the apex as well, perhaps with tie-bars linking the eaves. This metalwork can be painted to match the finish of the conservatory, or picked out in contrasting colour.

If the sides of the conservatory are un-glazed at the bottom, timber panelling can look attractive, and, if continued around to include the solid walls on conservatories built onto a house, can unify them visually with the glass ones. This effect may be enhanced by similarly extending the line of

OPPOSITE *This conservatory at Colney Hall, Norfolk, simply constructed in 1840 with a ridge roof behind a brick wall, is transformed by the use of a balustrade and classical detailing. This is stucco, cast and applied over the brickwork beneath.*

ABOVE *The pierced and carved bargeboards and the tall, turned, spiky finials of the new conservatory have been made to match the old ones on the roof above.*

Examples from Marston & Langinger's catalogue of traditional designs for windows and glazed doors.

the cornice across the top of the solid walls, and if the building is of a grander design – perhaps an orangery with columns or pilasters on the external sides – these, too, can be repeated internally on all the walls.

GLASS AND GLAZING

When the owners of Bicton Hall in Devon went to W. & D. Bailey in the early 1820s for a Palm House to be constructed in the gardens, they were ordering the most up-to-date design and technology then available. Today the design still has an impressively modern appearance, with its simple vertical bars and restrained decoration. The design was governed, however, by the type and dimensions of glass of the time. The glazing bars are closely spaced, and the curved roof shape takes advantage of the limited sizes of glass produced at that time. The curves on the roof are made by overlapping a series of flat panes to achieve the effect of bent glass.

The glass for Bicton would have been made by spinning a blob of molten glass on the end of a rod, until it formed a flat disc, four or more feet across, which was then allowed to cool. Panes were then cut from the perimeter, leaving the central bouillon, cheap panes which were sold to cottagers for windows and doors. (These whorled-glass panes may be seen today in the windows of modern homes whose owners are trying, mistakenly, for a Georgian appearance; no middle-class Georgian householder would have used them.) The small panes were glazed, overlapping like roof tiles, and the top and bottom were often cut to a curve, so that, as rainwater ran down the exterior, it was led to the centre of each pane and away from the glazing bars, thus reducing the risk of leaking and, it was thought, extending the life of the timber and putty.

Towards the 1850s a new technique of glass manufacture was developed: rolled glass, much cheaper and available in larger sizes. The result was a change in the design and construction of glass buildings and windows. For example, the eighteenth-century twelve-pane sash window started to disappear and was replaced by windows with sashes of only two, or even one, pane of glass each. The larger glass size discouraged the use of curved roofs in garden buildings, and consequently there was a move towards

RIGHT *Sam Deard's Patent Dry Glazing. The nineteenth century brought countless inventions and patents for glazing. This system offers bent roofs, achieved by dividing the curve into a series of flat facets.*

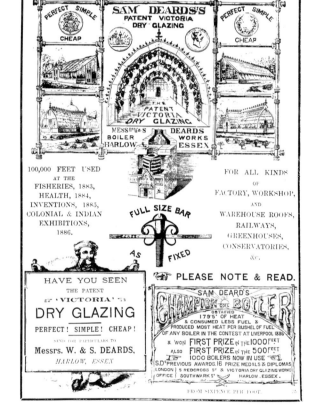

OPPOSITE *The removable double-glazing shown here is secured with beautifully carved timber clips. The soft cotton blinds are draped like sails from the ridge of the roof and held back at the eaves with hooks. The lower part, tied up here, can be let down to cover the windows.*

cheaper, straight timber glazing bars rather than cast- and wrought-iron glazing bars. The finest example from this period was the Great Exhibition Hall, the Crystal Palace, designed by Joseph Paxton for the 1851 Trade Fair held in Hyde Park. It measured 125 by 570 metres (400 by 1850 feet), and was built in ten months. Without sheet glass, it could never have been put up so quickly and so economically.

After more than a century, another revolution in the manufacture of glass, resulting from the invention of the float process in the 1960s, led to a further reduction in the price of glass and the introduction of new types of very high-quality glass being used for glass buildings; safety glass and sealed double-glazing are the two most obvious examples. It is these technical innovations which underline the changing fashions in conservatories, and which have made new uses possible today.

A heated, single-glazed conservatory provides a good environment for growing plants. Unfortunately the cold glass creates vast quantities of condensation, requiring special channels to remove the excess water. The high humidity associated with such rooms, though ideal for the growth of plants, is not comfortable for people, and the condensation channels let in draughts. Double-glazing, on the other hand, vastly reduces condensation and makes drainage unnecessary; therefore a double-glazed conservatory is much more comfortable, and less expensive to heat. In the 1990s double-glazing, in the form of sealed units, is the standard for all new glazing on windows and external doors, and is widely used in conservatories, particularly on roofs, where heat loss is considerable. A further development in double-glazing is the use of low-emissivity glass, usually called 'low E', which has a very thin layer of metallic oxides fused into the surface of one, or both, of the leaves of glass, resulting in a thermal efficiency equal to that of triple-glazing. It works rather like a thermos flask, trapping and reflecting radiated heat within the building.

The other major development in glazing is safety glass, which is made by two processes, tempering and laminating. Tem-

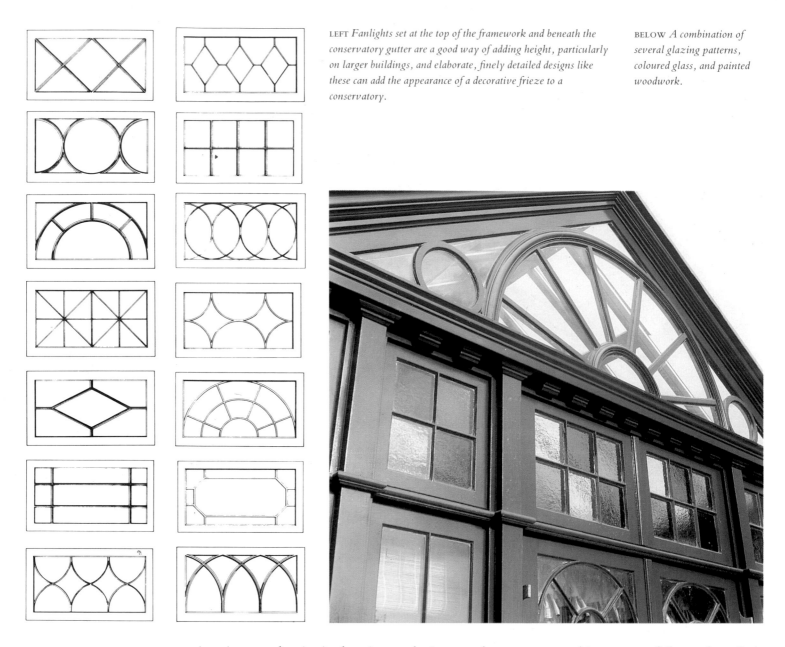

LEFT *Fanlights set at the top of the framework and beneath the conservatory gutter are a good way of adding height, particularly on larger buildings, and elaborate, finely detailed designs like these can add the appearance of a decorative frieze to a conservatory.*

BELOW *A combination of several glazing patterns, coloured glass, and painted woodwork.*

pering (or toughening) glass is a technique for increasing the strength of glass four- or five-fold, by heating the cut panes in a furnace, then cooling them very rapidly, so that the surface skin, cooling and hardening first, is left in tension, making the glass springy and impossible to crack in the ordinary way – if a pane is broken, it shatters into thousands of tiny glass beads. The alternative, laminated glass, consists of a tough, clear plastic inter-layer sandwiched between two thin panes of float glass. It is ideal for security because, although it cracks easily, it is very hard to break through.

Plastic glazing is promoted, particularly for roofs, because it is light and difficult to break, and, as it is now made in a honeycomb form, two or three layers thick, has excellent insulating qualities. However it is not attractive and, as it is soft enough to be scratched by atmospheric dust, will develop a milky appearance. Another problem,

An interesting combination of numerous styles of leaded stained glasswork including 'crazy paving' pattern and the date of the building. The craftsmanship of both the carpentry and glazing is of the highest standard.

created by its ability to expand and contract with changes in temperature, is a tendency to creak as it does so. This thermal movement also results in plastic glazing being much harder to make weatherproof, and, over time, it is susceptible to leaks.

In the past, before the advent of inexpensive toughening processes, wired glass was commonly used. Early versions were reinforced with chicken wire and generally had a rough surface, although the usual form sold today, Georgian wired, is clear and has a fine grid of wire reinforcement. Rather like laminated glass, it cracks easily, but is held together by the wire reinforcing. This feature makes it particularly good for situations where it is important to prevent fire spreading. This is the only inexpensive form of glazing available for this purpose. There are special, completely clear fireproof glasses on the market, usually laminated with a special fire-resistant plastic inter-layer, but these

117

ABOVE *A detail of a modern conservatory built by Marston & Langinger. The elaborately carved and moulded woodwork is glazed with leaded lights. At the centre of these are cut-glass stars – made by grinding away a surface coating of blue glass to expose the clear glass beneath. They are made in several colours and sizes.*

OPPOSITE *The granite sets used on the terrace taken up to build the conservatory have been reused inside to make a strong, trouble-free floor in keeping with the setting in the north of Scotland. The cast-iron underfloor heating grilles relieve the plainness of the random-sized slabs by creating a border for the floor design.*

materials are generally expensive and have to be ordered specially.

But glass, as well as being functional, can be used decoratively. Late Victorian and Edwardian conservatories were often decorated with coloured and etched glass, made up into patterns around the margins of doors and windows, or used as leaded patterns in rows of fanlights. Leaded lights are made by cutting out clear, obscure, or coloured glass in small pieces and assembling them over a full-size drawing of the design with cut and soldered lead, or occasionally fine brass jointing pieces, called cames. Leaded lights are often used in association with obscure glass, sand-blasted or etched into patterns reminiscent of net curtains with stars, diamonds, and fleurs-de-lys. A particularly beautiful form of decoration is created by coating ordinary glass with a thin layer of coloured glass (flashing) and then grinding and polishing the surface away to reveal the clear layer beneath, leaving patterns such as star-bursts and flowers. Many modern conservatories emulate this attrac-

tive form of decoration, using coloured glass in doors and windows to great effect to relieve an otherwise bland façade.

FLOORS

The floor is an integral part of a room and as important a part of it as any other aspect, yet is frequently neglected when a decorative scheme is being considered. Not only the look but also the feel and practicality of the flooring is critical. Its choice should be governed, like any other furnishing, by the use to which the room will ultimately by put. Whatever floor finishes are used in the adjoining house, there will almost certainly be a break and a change in style and material on entering a conservatory, a reminder that it is not just a house extension, but a different type of room. There are also practical considerations. Strong light (even north-facing conservatories will receive direct sunlight in summer) will fade carpets and cause timber floors to split and open the joints between boards. The ideal materials for a conservatory are those that are durable, remain unaffected by temperature or damp, and are easy to maintain: stone, terracotta, and ceramics, for instance. Old rugs however, are attractive, can be useful in relieving a hard floor, and generally make the room look more cosy. In some cases – for instance, if the room is to be used as an office – a solid floor may not be practical or desirable; in these rooms, linoleum, which is available in patterns and colours to suit all tastes, seagrass matting, now popularly used in many homes instead of carpet, or a linen floor may be better.

Earlier buildings had stone floors, simple flags roughly dressed or honed and close

YOUNG & MARTEN'S NEW DESIGNS FOR TESSELATED TILE PAVEMENTS.

STRATFORD, WALTHAMSTOW AND LEYTONSTONE.
205

ABOVE, LEFT AND RIGHT *Tile patterns.*

BELOW *A magnificent tiled floor from about 1860.*

ABOVE *A page from a catalogue dating from the early years of this century, by the builders' merchants Young & Marten. These beautiful, elaborate floors were very popular in hallways as well as in conservatories. They were generally laid with a border, sometimes with a central panel. There are now several companies producing similar products.*

jointed, perhaps with contrasting keys set into the corners, while more basic horticultural buildings might have had brick floors. The gothic revivals of the nineteenth century created an interest in medieval-style floors, made of small terracotta tiles of various colours arranged in patterns or encaustic tiles (with designs inlaid during manufacture). These were copied and developed to produce the wonderful, intricate, and colourful Victorian conservatory floors that came into vogue again in the 1980s.

The most popular flooring materials are terracotta tiles, usually 150 to 375 millimetres (6 to 16 inches) square, and, though traditional to England, imported from the Mediterranean. They vary in colour from light buff to dark red, and in texture from hard smooth and flat to soft rustic and quite uneven, but their success always depends on careful laying with the right pattern, small joints carefully pointed with the right colour mortar, and finishing with a specially formulated sealer. These tiles, which are made

without a finish, darken when sealed, and this should be taken into account when selecting them. Glazed floor tiles need no finishing and are made in a vast, subtle range of colours, but the glaze must meet a special flooring standard if they are to be so used and even so will eventually wear through to the terracotta beneath.

Natural materials suitable for conservatory floors are slate – solid black and green-grey or the Italian mottled type with attractive rust streaks; marble – black, white and many colours in between (with considerable variation in price); sandstone – cream, grey, or buff; and limestone, similar to sandstone but finer. All these materials can be combined with one another or with terracotta, to create patterns and borders, providing they are of similar thickness, and look very effective when used in this way. Slate and sandstone, typically York stone, can, if preferred, be laid with a riven, unhoned surface, for a country look, but it will be rough on furniture. Slate and marble can be

RIGHT *The gravel path outside this conservatory leads past the beautiful old brickwork of the house to a deodar and a view of the Buckinghamshire landscape beyond. The plain terracotta floor tiles have been laid to a diamond pattern to contrast with the border lined with slate.*

BELOW *The varnished, natural appearance of the wooden floor gives this conservatory a fresh, modern look.*

finely finished and polished, and are more appropriate in an urban setting. There are also a number of distinctive floors available from specialist suppliers; these use natural materials such as mosaic, terrazzo, and inlaid marble, and are made up into fashionable patterns.

Most of these materials will last as long as the structure, and because of this the design of the floor should be regarded, from the beginning, as part of the building. The colour, texture, size and pattern of laying and finish, together with a border and other devices, combine to make one of the most important features of interior decoration.

HEATING

Nineteenth-century advertisements for conservatories often seem to be as much about heating glasshouses as building them, with lots of claims by manufacturers about the reliability of their apparatus, assurances that they have never had a failure with 'their unsurpassed boilers and reliable pipework'. Indeed, a considerable part of the cost of building a conservatory would have been the construction of the boiler house, the underground duct-work, the elaborate system of hot-water pipes, the flues and chimneys, and storage for coal. The Victorians put considerable effort and ingenuity into the design of boilers, patenting a succession of inventions with names like the Gold Medal Boiler, the Improved Trentham, the Climax Saddle Boiler, and many others. This concern with heating was inevitable with buildings that were single-glazed, draughty, and not insulated. It was a time when house-owners were far less troubled by the cost or source of heating and happily consumed lorry-loads of coal to raise stove-houses to tropical temperatures.

Today, of course, such extravagant consumption of fuel is a thing of the past: very few people now attempt to maintain a minimum temperature for the growing of plants much above 60°F, or even 50°F, and buildings are much better insulated. It is now mandatory when building large structures with a floor of over 30 metres square (325 square feet), or for conservatories adjoining areas without connecting doors, to insulate to a very high standard with wall and underfloor insulation, double- or triple-glazing to windows, doors, and roof, and the use of special insulating glass. This meets the British Building Regulations requirements for heat conservation while retaining the appearance of a traditional building with clear-glass glazing. The floor should be insulated with a 50-millimetre (2-inch) layer of polystyrene foam set beneath the sand-and-cement screed; despite its apparent flimsiness this will support considerable weight because the pressure is spread through the floor and screed across the whole area of the insulation. It is now usual to construct walls with a cavity containing a layer of polystyrene insulation, but if the walls are to match existing brickwork they must be of the same type of brick, and laid in the same pattern. Doors and windows that fit tightly enough to cut off draughts will save energy. Draughtseals help as long as they are not readily visible; they should be renewable too. Unless the building is simply to be used as a greenhouse, double-glazing of the roof is essential, and, ideally should be fitted at the sides as well. Double-glazing does require much thicker glazing bars than single glass, and so it is important to bear this in mind if the doors and

windows have small panes, and the conservatory is to be built alongside windows with very fine glazing bars, as on a Regency house, for example. Triple-glazing, the ultimate in insulation, is sometimes used, although this is now being replaced by the introduction of low-emissivity glass, which if used in sealed units, made of double layers, and filled with argon gas, insulates as well as brickwork.

A selection of radiators from a catalogue by William Truswell & Son, The Architects Compendium, 1896.

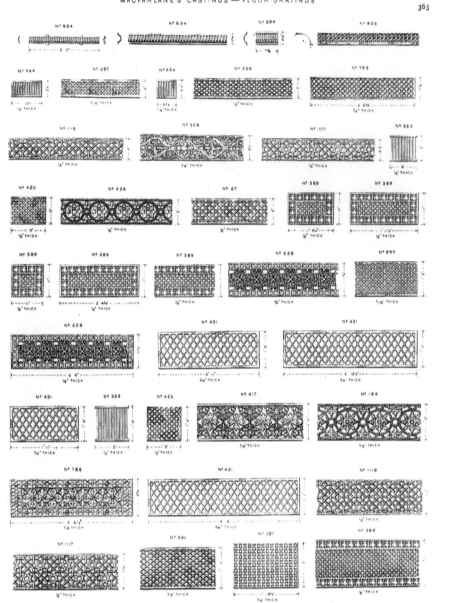

BELOW *Wollaton Hall Camellia House. Regency heating: warm air is ducted from a coal-fired boiler to the handsome bronze ventilator grilles set in the flagstone floor.*

ABOVE *Floor grilles provide drainage and cover underfloor heating pipes. Today they are usually associated with Victorian churches but they were commonly used in public buildings and private houses as well as greenhouses and conservatories. The gardener would hose through the grilles while the heating was on to create clouds of steam for the benefit of the plants. The top right-hand pattern is an interesting cover for heating pipes laid around a skirting.*

All this insulation has done away with the banks of pipes familiar from old greenhouses; all that is needed is a simple extension of the domestic central heating. It should have separate controls and, ideally, be piped direct from the boiler, so that it is possible for someone in the conservatory to operate the boiler independently at night, or whenever the other heating in the house is turned off. Traditional cast-iron radiators, with their substantial construction and high output, are a good choice; use low, deep models which can be fitted below windowsill level. An elegant alternative, and one that is ideal for conservatories, is underfloor pipes connected to the domestic central heating, set in a duct around the perimeter and covered with decorative cast-iron grilles. The special finned pipes emit a great deal of heat. They can go anywhere, even across doorways, and, of course, leave the floor and wall space clear.

Another method of underfloor heating is electric cables laid in sand, above the insulation, and arranged like the cables within an electric blanket, gently warming the floor above. This type of system can be connected to a time-switch to use low-cost electricity at

BELOW *Humid air rises from the heating pipes beneath immersed in a water channel, and passes through grilles of a particularly attractive Roman design. The cast iron grilles have been galvanised, preventing them from rusting, and giving them a colour which blends well with the stone floor.*

night. Economical and invisible, this is a practical form of heating, but it does tend to be inflexible, taking some time to adjust to changing weather and requirements.

It is also quite feasible to use an old-fashioned coal- or wood-fired cast-iron stove in a conservatory, but some plants will be susceptible to fumes, particularly from coal, and the temperature will fluctuate considerably. There are lots of models on the market, including a number of old, upright cylinder stoves, such as the Tortoise brand. If possible, they should be connected into an existing flue on the back wall of the room. A

new flue going up through the roof of a conservatory must be more than a foot or so in diameter to meet regulations, and have a metal jacket. Antique 'cathedral' stoves can sometimes be found; these are made from beautifully decorative cast iron in upright designs and contain a small oil heater which will shine prettily at night through the lacy sides of the stove. They will not, however, heat the room on their own.

These forms of heating are suitable for a conservatory which is used for both plants and people, but they may not be adequate for the more serious gardener. Commercial

ABOVE *A handsome oak radiator-case fitted just below window level, enabling it to double as a seat. Using the same material as the framework of the conservatory integrates the radiator and its case into the overall design of the building.*

*The owners of this first-floor
city conservatory wanted a
clean style for the interior and
used white cotton blinds for
the ceiling and traditional
timber venetian blinds with
pale-stained cedar slats for the
sides. The roller blinds on the
roof pull up only as far as the
electric motors which operate
the roof ventilators. It is
possible to fit blinds in this
position, but they would
have to be semi-fixed and
secured with clips.*

greenhouses are now usually warmed with heated air, ducted through pipes at roof level, and accurately controlled with thermostats. A similar arrangement will be necessary, although without the pipework of commercial buildings, if the conservatory covers a swimming pool. Poolhouses, unlike conservatories which need only the services of an ordinary plumber or heating engineer, require specialist advice and installation to prevent condensation and work properly.

SHADING

Unless the sun never catches the conservatory roof, some form of covering will be needed to keep the glasshouse from turning into a hothouse. The usual way to do this is with blinds, either on spring rollers or folded, Roman style. Wooden venetian blinds can also be used, some of which are specially manufactured for fitting into roofs, and can be electrically operated. They give the room a modern, formal look, especially suitable if it is to be used as an office or study.

Blinds are most effective, and look best, when fitted to the entire roof area, although roof ventilators must usually be left clear. They are sometimes fitted on doors and windows as well, but for the purpose of providing privacy rather than shade. The traditional material for conservatory blinds is pinoleum – pinewood sawn into matchstick-size reeds, laid side by side and sewn together, and finished with cloth-bound edges. It filters approximately two-thirds of the sun and, as it is stiff across its width, is less likely to sag than other materials. An alternative is Holland cloth, which is stiffened by being treated with starch and preservative; this has a lighter appearance, and is particularly suitable for a conservatory used as an additional room, with few plants. Both pinoleum and Holland blinds can be shaped to fit awkward angles in roofs. There are also a number of plastic materials available, some with a metallic outer face to reflect the sun.

A more informal and slightly exotic effect can be created by fixing a fine, soft fabric in a natural fibre, such as muslin or cheesecloth, to the highest point of the conservatory, then draping it, tent-fashion, against the sides. You will not, however, be able to raise or lower it, and this type of shading requires more frequent cleaning than conventional blinds.

Curtains are occasionally hung in conservatories used more for sitting or dining rather than as garden rooms. They are usually fitted in pairs looped back against the posts between the windows, perhaps with the same fabric gathered and stretched between cords in the roof. Special modification to the framework will, in most cases, be needed to make room for the tracks and other fittings and to cover them neatly. The fabrics must be specially selected to withstand the bleaching of sunlight and humidity. Rather like fitted carpets in a conservatory, the use of curtains is at odds with the style of such rooms, and they should be used only where a cosy atmosphere is considered more important than a verdant one.

Outside the conservatory roof, technically sophisticated venetian blinds can also be installed. Permanently fitted, they can be installed to operate electrically, adjusting the angle of the slats automatically to the sun.

ABOVE *Pinoleum roof blinds. Manufactured in France on ancient, unique looms, from cotton and timber specially grown and cut into reeds in Romania, pinoleum provides ideal shading. This example is particularly attractive in traditional dark green, matching the colour of the conservatory.*

LEFT *The roof blinds are tightly pleated to concertina up and down the roof in tracks fixed to the underside of the glazing bars. They are suitable only for square or rectangular roofs. The curtains have the matching fabric fixed around the pole.*

although deciduous, will cut out most of the sun from May to September, the period when shading for other plants is critical.

A conservatory that will be continually subjected to very strong sunlight can incorporate some shading in the structure by substituting a solid material for some of the glazing panels in the roof. This works particularly well if the conservatory adjoins another structure on two or more sides as the unglazed sections will not be plainly visible from the outside. Conventional roofing material appropriate to the rest of the building is probably best.

VENTILATION

More than any other type of room, a conservatory needs ventilation. This is especially important for successfully growing plants, but even without them it is still

ABOVE While this roof has traditional conservatory blinds, curtains with a frilly pelmet have been added below for a cosy sitting-room atmosphere.

RIGHT Doors that can be folded and hooked back are a huge help in warm weather. A through draft, coupled with roof blinds, will be very effective in controlling the temperature.

Buildings with simple ridge or lean-to roofs, requiring only rectangular, untapered blinds and used for growing plants can be shaded with external blinds made of laths of cedarwood linked together and fitted to roll up and down from the ridge. These are very attractive and long-lasting and, as they are outside, permit climbers to be trained up the interior of the roof. Outside the conservatory as well, deciduous climbers may be trained over the roof for shade, though care must be taken that they do not grow so luxuriantly that they block the light or endanger guttering and ornament. In the first few seasons, of course, another form of shading must be used until they reach their full growth. Rooftop plants are good for the other plants, as well as the people, inside: a grapevine trained over the roof for example,

necessary to be able to cool the building in summer. There are a number of ways in which this can be done. Some of the windows can be made to open, doors can be fixed open, fanlights can be fitted beneath the eaves, and ventilators at the ridge of the roof.

If the conservatory is built against a north-facing wall, and receives little or no sun, there is still the need for a few windows that can be opened, which, together with a roof ventilator, will be adequate. If the building receives lots of sun, especially if it is against a south-facing wall, considerable ventilation will be required, with openings at top and bottom, so that a draught is created, with the warm air naturally rising up through the building to escape at the ridge of the roof.

As a rule, it should be possible to open approximately a third of the windows, although practical considerations of their arrangement in the building, and whether

The antique dealer who owns this conservatory found and had restored an old ceiling fan which, in combination with the beautiful dark-green pinoteum blinds, huge double doors and roof ventilators, ensures a pleasant temperature whatever the weather.

their opening would cause an obstruction, need to be considered. Vertically sliding sashes or centre-pivoted windows are best, as they can be opened at top and bottom at the same time. However, sash windows are expensive to construct, and pivoting windows can be inconvenient, especially as they are usually arranged so that the top opens inwards, and this may get in the way of blinds or planting. Side-hung windows are simple and traditional, but not advisable if they are big or heavy (double-glazing will add considerably to the weight), and this is particularly true in a windy location, where they can easily swing loose if a firm grip is not kept on the handle when opening them.

Windows hinged at the top and opening out are probably the simplest solution, providing ventilation from the bottom where it is most needed. They are safe from the risk of being caught in the wind, and, if left open in the rain, will not allow it to enter unless driven by the wind.

Doors opening onto a terrace are particularly useful for providing large amounts of ventilation on a hot day. They should be hung on hinges that permit them to be folded outwards through 180°, so that they can be hooked back against the frame of the conservatory or adjacent walls. This has the added advantage of helping to unify the terrace with the interior of the conservatory.

Roof ventilation is essential in all but the smallest, most shaded buildings, and should be provided as high up as possible. Older horticultural glasshouses were fitted with banks of hinged ventilators along the top of the roof, or occasionally had huge, counterbalanced sliding sashes up and down the exterior of the roof. These ventilators were controlled by a variety of Heath Robinson devices for opening and closing them with levers, rods, cords and chains, pulleys and weights, typical of Victorian inventiveness. However, the ventilators tended to be leaky and were certainly not draughtproof, whereas modern systems are expected to be completely weathertight, while at the same time having a neat appearance. They are generally specially constructed windows, hinged from the ridge of the roof and protected from the rain and wind with specifically designed flashings and seals. They are usually opened and shut with a screw-operated opener turned by a pole with a hook at the end which engages in the bottom of the screw, or by a cord-and-pulley system. More sophisticated openers

are electrically operated, and some companies provide thermostats and automatic control equipment. The simple mechanisms designed for greenhouses, which work automatically with a cylinder filled with wax of a very high thermal expansion and contraction, are unsuitable. They are usually not strong enough to operate the larger double-glazed ventilators used in conservatory roofs, and, because these buildings are generally higher, cannot be easily reached for adjustment. Furthermore, there is no way of making them open or shut manually. Another system sometimes offered involves a series of louvres at the ridge, operated by the wax-type openers, which work more satis-

A tall bay-ended conservatory with a lantern, timber-ridge cresting, and a finial to emphasize the shape of the roof suits the solid Victorian family house to which it is attached. Doors lead into the kitchen, drawing room, and, down the re-used stone steps, to the garden. The windows are hinged from the top.

131

factorily in this way. If the conservatory has a lantern with glazed sides at the top of the roof, these can be made to open with either electric motors, or a cable system, to provide excellent high-level ventilation. Fans will also help by circulating the air and drawing it upwards. Propeller-types are quiet and

RIGHT *Condensation depends on many factors: the difference between the inside and outside temperature, the insulating quality of the glass, the humidity of the air inside, and the degree of movement of the air. A building would be most susceptible to condensation if it is single glazed and, as here, has many plants in beds.*

attractive. It is occasionally possible to buy secondhand 'colonial' fittings, but check that they are electrically safe, otherwise new fittings in modern or reproduction styles are readily available.

FAR RIGHT *An electrified reproduction of a candle bracket with a condensing reflector of tiny silver and glass facets.*

Cooling

In places that are very hot in summer, ventilation and shading may not be enough. Air conditioning, either with a simple refrigerating unit or more complicated equipment which recirculates the air controlling the humidity, can be used; but the apparatus can be bulky, unattractive, and noisy. If there are convenient solid walls it can be set into them, or behind them and connected with a duct. Do not install the high-level ducts commonly used in commercial build-

ings, public swimming pools, and the like, as these are quite inappropriate for domestic use. More expensive underfloor ducts, with the cooled air rising up through grilles, are very effective and unobtrusive but will require a consultant on air conditioning to be called in at the beginning of the project.

If the size, and situation, of the conservatory does not warrant an air conditioner, make sure there are plenty of openable windows and doors, and high-level ventilation arranged to create plenty of cross-draughts, together with a ceiling blind and fan or fans.

LIGHTING

Designed to let in light during the day, glass buildings also let most of it out at night. In general, a number of low-intensity lights – the sort that would be used for illuminating the garden itself – give a softer, more

LEFT *A large brass lantern in the roof of the conservatory at Ettington Park, now a hotel. This type of lamp, glazed and designed to offer some protection from wind and rain, is particularly suitable in a conservatory.*

appropriate effect than a few bright ones. Keep in mind the difference between light-ing a glass room and one with solid walls – there will be no benefit from light reflected off ceilings and walls, as in an ordinary room, but there will, on the other hand, be the risk of harsh reflections from strong lights. Do not, for instance, use uplighters; these will bounce back glaring spots from the roof panes.

Nineteenth-century garden rooms were lit with oil lamps and candle light, with Chinese lanterns for parties, and later, when gas, and then electricity, came into use, with decorative brass and glass wall brackets and hanging lamps. All these lighting techniques can be adapted to the modern conservatory. Antique, reproduction, or modern wall brackets can be fixed to the solid wall of a

LEFT *Reproduction Moorish-style lamps. This traditional design, with its miniature geometric glass construction, is excellent for a conservatory roof.*

conservatory that adjoins a house. Candles are the ideal form of lighting – though not the most practical method for everyday use, they can give the conservatory a romantic and mysterious look for a special occasion. A variety of coloured and patterned candles can be set in glass holders. Simple night lights in coloured pressed-glass shades can be placed on any narrow space or suspended from a wire. Larger ones, in brass, glass, or china, candlesticks, or enclosed in glass hurricane shades, can go on a table, or they can be put in brass wall brackets or lanterns or a chandelier. Remember, the great advantage of candlelight is its flexibility.

Halogen (low-voltage) lighting fitted with a dimmer produces the same warm glow as candlelight and, installed correctly, can be quite unobtrusive. Low-voltage lamps are available in very small sizes (with a separate hidden transformer operating a group), and can be fitted high in the roof, where they are barely visible, to spotlight the room below. Conventional spotlamps are really too large and the wrong style for most conservatories. Ordinary hanging lamps with globe or clear-glass shades will provide general lighting, particularly in larger buildings, but if blinds are fitted, care must be taken to ensure that one does not obstruct the other. A chandelier hanging from the apex of the roof or lantern makes a grand centrepiece. Designs in glass with clear or coloured drops and strings of glass beads, wrought iron (particularly Arts and Crafts examples with naturalistic leaves, fruit and tendrils), and brass or bronze patterns are all appropriate.

When preparing a lighting plan, always allow for the possibility of the furniture and planting being rearranged. If plants thrive and grow large this will be essential. Lighting points, positioned 30 to 40 centimetres (a foot or so) above floor level so they can be reached easily and kept dry, can be installed around the room and controlled by a switch at the entrance. It should be possible to wire points for lamps (and fans) in the roof without the wiring being visible. Outside lights are useful, especially if there is a terrace and paths around the building, both for evening entertainment in the garden and for enjoyment of the garden from the conservatory. Light fittings can be attached to the main posts, or mullions, of the framework, a little below the gutter and can be discreet or a feature in their own right.

LEFT AND ABOVE *Conservatories look magical at night when viewed from the outside. The small late-Victorian conservatory* (above), *built by Boulton & Paul, is lit by small brass paraffin lamps and candles.*

6

DRESSING THE SPACE

FURNITURE, STATUARY AND ORNAMENT

FURNITURE

OPPOSITE *A very tall
conservatory, designed and
built by Marston &
Langinger, with a lantern
along the apex of the roof. A
first-floor window on the
house staircase opens into the
roof. The interior, furnished
with an eclectic assortment of
antiques, has a riven slate
floor sealed to bring out the
natural dark colour. In the
background is a tall
papyrus plant.*

Robust materials with easily maintained finishes that age attractively
are best for conservatory furniture. Slate and marble, cast and
wrought iron, wicker and natural timber, cottons and linens are all
ideal. Polished wood and materials that are affected by damp or
bright light should be avoided, and this generally means using matt
or textured finishes rather than glossy, polished ones. Painted
furniture is best of all. It wears well, is colourful, and has the
informal, cheerful style appropriate in a conservatory.

At least one large table will almost certainly be needed, with
a top of clear or frosted glass, slate – either black or grey-green
– marble, granite or perhaps slatted wood or even steel. A heavy
material, such as slate or glass, simply rests on the base, which
could be of cast or wrought iron, polished steel, or painted
metal. A wooden top, though, should have a wooden base.
Tough varieties, such as oak or teak, which age attractively, are
best. Side tables can be of cane or willow wicker with tops of
the same material, sometimes with a sheet of glass over them
to provide a flatter surface, and cast-iron or painted-steel tables can
introduce variety and colour. An alternative is to cover a simple
wooden table with a woven or printed cloth, such as a hand-blocked
Indian or Provençal print, but do keep in mind the bleaching effect of
light on the pattern and colour.

The best type of chairs for use in a conservatory are a cross
between dining and garden seats, the first being generally too formal,
and the second too bulky. It is better to select chairs which have some
association with the garden or veranda – they don't have to match.
Painted wooden chairs with seagrass or rush seats are fine, perhaps

Garden room furniture from Harrods' Brushes and Turnery Department Catalogue, 1905.
TOP RIGHT *An upholstered wicker settee, then the height of fashion. Cane and rush furniture was also popular, and could be covered in cretoune, tapestry or genoa velvet.* RIGHT *A rattan easy chair. The conservatory furniture of this era displays great ingenuity and inventiveness with the use of chain, ring, diaper and other woven patterns.*

BELOW *Two small cast-iron tables from the Edwardian catalogue of Young & Marten, East London Merchants & Manufacturers. These designs were offered unfinished, painted, or with a choice of bronzed metalwork, with mahogany or Sicilian marble tops, at prices from 7s/6d to 21s.*

with tie-on cushions, but polished wood is not appropriate. Not only does it look out of place, it will deteriorate in the moisture and sunlight of a conservatory, and is likely to be damaged by an uneven floor. There is a long tradition of wicker chairs in garden rooms. Considerable ingenuity has been used for over two hundred years in their design, whether made of willow, Filipino rattan, round or split cane, or combined with bamboo (real or imitation). Lloyd loom chairs in designs of the 1920s and 1930s are available now in a wide range of colours and finishes. Secondhand ones are usually painted eau-de-nil, or, less attractively, gold, but can easily be repainted. Lloyd loom, introduced into England in 1922, is manufactured to a patented technique, spinning paper around steel wire, then treating and painting it, to produce surprisingly strong and long-lasting furniture. The designs of the 1920s and 1930s were very popular, so much original furniture is available.

There are lots of attractive chair designs in polished, galvanised, or painted steel, formed from wire, bars, or straps, and constructed with impressive ingenuity, but never buy a chair without trying it to make sure it is comfortable, as appearance is frequently misleading. Another thing to be aware of with steel, particularly if it is polished, is that it can suffer from rust, which will destroy cushions.

Cast iron is ideal for occasional chairs and benches. The picturesque style of early Victorian times produced some extraordinary designs in cast iron, imitating nature with knotty branches made to look like crude rustic work, ivy, ferns, acanthus leaves, or vines with bunches of grapes or other fruit. Antique dealers and salerooms regularly have Victorian cast iron, but check for fractures that may be covered by paint – they will be very difficult to repair. For seating around a table, cast iron is too heavy, but inexpensive cast-aluminium chairs which are much lighter are available generally in fancy Victorian patterns.

For chairs to relax in – sofas, armchairs

LEFT *This conservatory has been decorated predominantly in green and orange with a scagliola-topped table and Citrus mitis in pots. The wicker chair, an usual combination of rattan cane on an iron frame, is very light and strong. In the background are banana palms and papyrus to the right of the wrought-iron candelabra.*

Designs for a large wicker sofa and side table. Wicker furniture is especially suitable for use in the conservatory and is little affected by sun and damp.

and chaises longues – wicker is the best material. Its informal style is right for a conservatory, it is strong enough to stand up to sunlight and humidity, and it can be left out all summer without suffering. Wicker is traditionally made from witheys, the shoots that grow up to 2.5 metres (8 feet) each year on pollarded willows, planted in damp

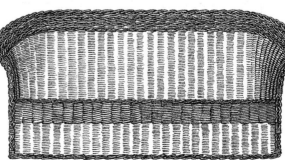

OPPOSITE *The interior of this Marston & Langinger conservatory has been furnished with a richly coloured assortment of woven and printed textiles by decorator Ruth Barclay.*

LEFT *This small conservatory, built to enclose a recess of a tiny Thames-side house, makes a pretty place to sit amongst the flowers.*

BELOW *Steel is excellent for conservatory furniture but needs to be either painted or, as in this case, lacquered to prevent rust. This modern comfortable easy chair is designed to take a full length tie-on cushion.*

regions, such as Sedgemoor in Somerset, or the Broads in Norfolk. The shoots are stripped of their leaves and thin bark (a procedure that gave rise to the folk dance 'strip the willow'), dried, and then woven into chairs, tables, and baskets. Nineteenth-century examples, though rare now, are sometimes very elaborate with curlicues and pierced work in the decoration. (They are still manufactured in small quantities in this style in Madeira, where the willows are grown in small terraced paddies.) Victorian wickerwork was usually upholstered with tight-fitting cushions, sometimes stitched into the backs, and with coverings of thick materials such as plush or old cut-down Oriental rugs. Modern furniture generally has cushions filled with feather or down,

The conservatory at Bromley Hill, Kent, as painted by John Chessel Buckler. At the bottom of the almost opaque canopy of climbers is a beautiful collection of Chinese seats and pots, with smaller pots lining the stairs that lead to the classically decorated interior of the house.

and their design can be ornamented with decorative brackets at the top of the legs. The space beneath can be used for radiators or filled in with panelling and doors to make the most of the space for storage, often a problem in conservatories.

Transferring a newly bought specimen from its plastic container to an attractive ceramic pot will immensely improve the appearance of a plant, even if the substitute is only an ordinary terracotta flowerpot. Although the difference will at first seem esoteric, old hand-thrown clay flowerpots are undoubtedly the best, as they are well proportioned and have a subtly shaped lip; they should be bought whenever the opportunity arises, as, with time and breakages, they become rarer. There are now a few craftsmen producing good-quality, hand-thrown pots, generally with additional decoration, such as handles, crimped edges, and incised friezes. There are also lots of glazed pots, imported from Spain and Portugal, Italy and the South of France, as well as from China, where they are usually made with a deep green or blue glaze. Make sure they they have drainage holes if plants are to be put into them. Otherwise, choose watertight glazed ones, and use them with a plastic or zinc liner. The latter are easy to have made up.

Beautifully decorated Chinese pots up to 800 millimetres (2 feet 8 inches) in diameter have been used for many years for specimen trees and shrubs, such as camellias, palms, and tree ferns. Originally made as an alternative to barrels for the storage and export of 100-year-old eggs, they were coated with pale blue or green glaze inside and, generally, a dull olive-green outside, and decorated with hand-painted yellow or brown dragons and other Chinese motifs. They are

fitted with loose covers. It may be left in the natural blond or buff colour, or painted. Considerable quantities of rattan-cane furniture is produced in the Far East, particularly in the Philippines and Indonesia, and finished in the natural brown colour, painted, or, more recently, given a large variety of distressed finishes.

PLANT HOLDERS

Traditional staging for potted plants can be adapted to provide bench seats with cushions over a slatted top. They need to be built lower than the usual height for plants, 400 to 500 millimetres (16 to 20 inches) high,

now manufactured in a range of sizes for the European and North American market specifically for use as ornamental plant pots.

For a formal effect, the classic plantholders are Versailles tubs – wooden, square, with turned balls on the corners and boarded sides. The early versions, designed to carry trees or shrubs back and forth between the orangery and terrace each season, had hooks or rings on opposite sides, to slide poles

A carefully restricted colour range – white, blue-greens and grey-greens – was selected for the decoration of this conservatory. The floor and heating grilles have been incorporated into the scheme. The green wire jardinière (see design left) has green-and-white ivies and white pelargoniums, and next to it is a beautiful green-streaked amphora.

143

Ordinary clay pots may be decorated with shells to make an unusual plant container.

OPPOSITE *Interior of the conservatory at Flintham Hall. This extraordinary Victorian building has survived because, although it has all the elaborate rich decoration typical of wood or iron construction, it is built of stone. A balcony gives a view down from the first-floor library. A finely carved fountain adorned with shells, acanthus leaves, and serpents dominates the interior, which also includes an excellent collection of hanging baskets, Victorian statuary, a grand cast-iron settee, trellises, and lot of plants.*

Inexpensive wooden tubs can hold even the largest plant, such as these cycads — primitive, fern-like plants. Above them wire baskets are hung from the roof tie-bar. (Check before doing this that the bar will support their weight.)

through, so that, with one man on each corner, quite large orange trees could easily be moved. They derive their name from the ones still used at Versailles, where the largest contain tall palm trees. Modern examples are generally smaller, without lifting hooks, and are painted white, but they are also attractive in dark green and terracotta. They are best used with a liner to protect the timber, unless they are of a durable hardwood, such as teak or iroko, in which case they are usually left natural, or have an oiled finish.

Jardinières made from a stiff wire frame, reinforced with decorative curlicues and criss-crosses of wire, have for a long while been used to display potted plants in a group for a bold and instant floral effect that, unlike a potted border or staging, can be moved about. They are very decorative and are made in numerous pretty designs, from small ones that hold a single pot to elaborate semi-circular models, tiered like a wedding cake. In a large conservatory a pair of semi-circular wire jardinières, set back to back and filled with plants, with a large and impressive one at the top, make a very fine central display. It is a good plan to have metal liners made for them to catch any water that drips through the pots when watering. The same method of construction is used for making wire hanging baskets, available in plain dish shapes or decorated patterns with lacy edges and other ornamental work. They should be neatly lined with sphagnum moss and carefully filled when planting so they look attractive from beneath. Be careful with the larger sizes, as they can be extremely heavy when planted out, needing an arrangement of pulleys and a cleat for raising, lowering and securing them.

STATUARY

Plants and furniture are, of course, the most important aspects of decoration in the conservatory, but there is also a place in it for art. There is a long tradition of statuary in garden rooms. The fashion for ornaments of

this type first came from Italy; statues were bought during the Grand Tour and brought back for English gardens, where marble and alabaster fared better under glass, away from frost, and later, since Victorian times, from air pollution. In fact, there is some evidence that Georgian orangeries were sometimes used partly as sculpture galleries, and made good settings for figures of shepherds, shepherdesses, and Pomona. From this period a huge variety of marble and other stone statues exists, as does cast leadwork, which, when well done, is very attractive. The Victorians favoured white marble and alabaster, which were ideal for the romantic, partially draped nude ladies set amongst the palm and fern fronds. There are very good examples in Scotland at the Kibble Palace in Glasgow, well worth a visit not just for its statuary but for its impressive futuristic geometrical architecture. In a modern conservatory of restrained design, a delicate piece of abstract sculpture might be appropriate.

Statuary can be mounted on brackets, fitted to the solid walls, mounted on plinths,

LEFT *Cast-stone fountain spouts in the form of grotesque heads. A fountain, even if only of lightly trickling water, creates a pleasant sound and provides humidity in a conservatory. The water is re-circulated with an electric pump hidden in the wall or beneath the floor.*

LEFT *Longwood Gardens. The conservatory is part of an estate built as a country home for Pierre S. du Pont, a former chairman of both General Motors and the Dupont Corporation. It is now open to the public, and the impressive conservatory, with its pool fountain, lush planting, and statuary may be visited. The hanging pelargonium in the centre is particularly fine.*

or used as the centrepiece of a pond or a fountain. There are lots of fountains available in bronze which look wonderful with verdigris stone, real or reconstituted, and majolica. These usually take the form of grotesque human or lion heads with open jaws from which the water spouts, dolphins and fishes, ladies endlessly pouring water from a vase or the inevitable but charming putti. The installation of these can be quite complicated, involving a properly water-proofed base or pool and an electric recir-culating pump (*not* mains water and a drain). Apart from the pleasure of the statuary, the sound of trickling water will always contri-bute to a gentle and peaceful atmosphere.

7

GARDENING IN THE CONSERVATORY

GENERAL CONSIDERATIONS

For anybody, whether gardener or not, living in a temperate climate, it is a great pleasure in the depths of winter to step into a heated glasshouse filled with lush, growing plants and the scent of blossom. Being in a room of fresh, green, new growth, flowering bulbs, and a mist of white jasmine while outside the world is dormant, frosty, and leafless is a deeply romantic experience. This contrast particularly appealed to Victorian attitudes and tastes in a colonial era, when distant and dangerous exploration was continually bringing back to Europe strange new plants and animals. The excitement of building with the daring new techniques of prefabricated cast iron and glass, coupled with a desire to conserve these novelties of natural history, resulted in the construction of vast structures of completely original design, heated to high temperatures regardless of cost. Sadly, almost none of the privately built 'stove' houses survives with its tropical interior intact, but many of the large public conservatories are still maintained. The Great Palm House at Kew, planted with a huge, exotic collection including 20-metre (60-foot) palm trees, was maintained at a tropical heat even in the deepest winter snow from its erection in 1848 to 1988, when it was closed for refurbishment (it is now beautifully restored and replanted). Most new conservatories are not designed to house a steamy rain forest, but, with modest heating, can sustain a wide range of tender plants.

It soon becomes apparent to anybody growing plants under glass that the ideal environment for, say, a grapevine will not be the right one for gardenias, which, in turn, would not suit an orange tree. The vastly varying cultural requirements of plants is displayed in the Princess of Wales Conservatory at Kew. This modern, cleverly

OPPOSITE *Rockwood House, Wilmington, Delaware. The conservatory, which adjoins the main house, was inspired by the late-nineteenth-century aesthetic movement. The design of the structure is loosely based on Jacobean features and has mock hammer-beam roof trusses with a colour scheme of mauvish-beige, stone, and pale yellow, which, for a conservatory, must be unique.*

conceived (but architecturally uninspiring) building contains ten climates, from cold desert to tropical rain forest, and demonstrates to the conservatory gardener selecting plants the importance of deciding which type of habitat is possible for his situation and which style of planting most appropriate to it. Many plants, of course, require conditions that are quite unsuitable for furnishings and people, so it is important not to be unrealistic when choosing plants for the conservatory.

Light

No matter what choices are made about the selection of plants, the way in which they are displayed, and the humidity and temperature range, the most important factor will be the amount of sunlight available, and this will depend largely on the position of the building. Commercial greenhouses are generally put up on open sites and designed to admit maximum light (controlled in summer with whitewash). Most conservatories are built with architectural considerations foremost, and are often attached to houses that receive relatively little light. This should not, however, be automatically considered a disadvantage. A naturally shaded north-facing conservatory will encourage the growth of foliage and, protected from the sun, will have a relatively even temperature; it will be an ideal room in which to grow ferns to huge sizes in pots, hanging baskets, or beds. A conservatory built against the north side of a house will, however, receive some direct sun at midday, particularly between May and August, unless the wall behind is especially high. If the building faces south, the amount of sunlight will almost certainly make shading essential,

This large conservatory photographed in January shows the importance of variety in leaf texture and colour.

The Great Palm House, Kew. Only a public institution can justify the cost of maintaining this steaming rain-forest climate. The constant high temperature and humidity has produced the growth seen here within two years of reopening the building after complete refurbishment.

but it will encourage blossom and lend itself to an informal atmosphere; conversely, buildings with a northerly aspect are more appropriately treated in a formal manner.

Temperature

Nearly all modern conservatories have double-glazed roofs, at least one side of masonry or brick, and, usually, double glazing on the remaining sides and draught-

seals around the doors and windows. With the weather so effectively kept out, they are much easier to heat than the simple greenhouse, making it practical for the serious gardener to grow plants such as stephanotis or gardenias. The problems come with the need to accommodate, at the same time, other uses for the space and the needs of people, together with the right heating system. If you go for a high all-year-round temperature with lots of plants, the room will be too humid for people to spend much time there; furniture may suffer, and any books or magazines left behind certainly will. In most cases, a conservatory is heated by an extension of the domestic central-heating system. Unless a special arrangement is made with a thermostat and controller to turn the system on for the conservatory at night (while it is off for the rest of the house), it will be too cold in winter for many plants to survive. The most common and understandable mistake is attempting to grow plants which require a minimum temperature which cannot be maintained: specimens barely survive winter, fail to recover properly in spring, and eventually succumb to disease. This is not necessary, as there is a vast range of interesting and unusual plants that can be grown with very little heat. To succeed, first consider the other uses of the room. Is it to be used for eating (and, if so, how often)? Will it be used for entertaining, or simply to disappear into, to curl up and read amongst the plants? Then decide on the style and quantity of planting desirable, the highest minimum temperature which can easily be maintained (with, say, 5 degrees of frost outside) and tolerated, and then select plants which can not only survive but flourish in such conditions.

PLANT COLLECTIONS

The conservatory may be a link between the house and the garden, but it will have a style all its own, and this will be derived from the location, the architecture, the way in which the room is used, the furnishings, and the plants that live in it. You might have a formal garden room with a cool, ordered

and symmetrical interior, decorated with formal tubs containing well-shaped camellias, citrus fruit, or palms, or it may be more of a greenhouse, with an old sofa amongst the seed trays, overrun with an old vine, climbing jasmine, or self-seeded ferns. Unlike an outside garden, it will be much easier to rearrange from season to season, or as your moods and interests change, if most of the plants are grown in pots. In almost every case, however, there will be one or

Gunton Hall conservatory. Despite having no heating, its plants are thriving in an East Anglian midwinter. As the camellias finish, the jasmine growing up into the roof will start to flower.

ABOVE Deciduous shading. Annual climbers such as Cobaea scandens, *or* ipomoea *(seen here) can cover a conservatory roof within a season. This variety, 'Heavenly Blue', is very beautiful, but only one of many ipomoeas available as seeds or seedlings.*

OPPOSITE Plumbago at Clinton Lodge. This beautiful Mediterranean climber produces abundant scentless blossom in spring and summer, with flowers of unique grey-blue. There is also a white variety.

bago, and datura plants, however tempting they may look in a Mediterranean market, will languish on English and more northerly American windowsills and eventually die. Building a conservatory provides the opportunity to assuage a passion for acquiring tender and exotic plants. In no time at all the space will be filled with pots and trays of cuttings and seedlings, which before long develop into large plants fighting for space. In a season a young vine or passionflower can cover the roof, and a banana plant bought in a 15-centimetre (6-inch) pot may reach 3 metres (10 feet). It is quite easy within eighteen months to find that the chairs placed in the middle of the room to enable you to enjoy a plant collection can no longer be reached, and the table has become staging for pots because it is the only place left for them.

As with any gardening, it is essential to be ruthless. When a specimen becomes too big, it must be pruned or given away. It is far too easy to be sentimental with a collection of hard-won or expensive plants, and to become chained to a demanding regime of staggered feeding and watering schedules, constantly having to rearrange specimens as they grow, to cope with varying requirements of light and shade, dryness and humidity. A plant collection should be easy to cope with. Space should be allowed around plants so they receive sufficient light and so they can be easily watered, sprayed, and fertilised. If there are too many plants, it is surprisingly easy to lose them behind overhanging foliage only to discover them months later, dry and dead. Group the collection according to the orientation of the building, so those needing light are at the front, and shade-lovers are at the back or sheltered from direct sun by other plants.

two large varieties planted in the ground, or established in an ancient tub, that will set the style of the room. For a perfect display, it greatly helps to have a separate greenhouse to care for sickly specimens, store bulbs and tubers when dormant, and grow seedlings and cuttings. It is surprising how many fine shows of conservatory plants depend on such an arrangement.

All of us, if we are enthusiastic gardeners, will have seen plants in our travels abroad, or come across ones in catalogues or books that we long to grow but which are too delicate for the garden or would require too much heat in a greenhouse. Bougainvillea, plum-

RIGHT *Traditional grotto at Colney Hall, Norfolk.*

Move pots around, studying how each plant grows until the ideal position is found. Make sure there is a balanced selection, with climbers and baskets high up, shrubs and bigger specimens at eye level, and small plants and ground cover at the bottom.

Making a plant collection in a conservatory becomes considerably simpler if the selection is restricted to particular types and cultural requirements. Using, for example, plants found in the Mediterranean, such as bougainvillea, mimosa, and agapanthus, with their sunny associations and colourful blossom, gives a definite style to the planting, and simplifies the cultural requirements – moderate humidity, and 10°C (50°F) minimum temperature. Bear in mind that lots of plants of this type are deciduous, and do not look good in winter, so a proportion of evergreen specimens (lots of plants which lose their leaves in winter outdoors keep them in the milder climate of the conservatory) may be needed to provide interest throughout the year.

Hothouses

Private hothouses are now rare and generally confined to botanical gardens, where the hothouse provides part of a range of tropical and sub-tropical habitats. The most exotic climate achieved under glass must be that of the tropical rain forest requiring high temperatures day and night throughout the year and virtually hundred-percent humidity. This is achieved in older buildings with ranks of hot-water pipes and a floor of cast-iron grilles through which steam rises from heated water channels beneath. Daily or twice-daily damping down with a hosepipe, wetting the floors and foliage, is essential to maintain the conservatory atmosphere.

New buildings have radiators or warm-air heating, combined with automatic misting equipment. The conditions achieved in this way enable the most extraordinary and lush plants to be grown, most of which are too specialized to be within the scope of this book. They include palms, bromeliads (such as pineapples), orchids, tropical ferns, and bananas, which will bear fruit within a year in such conditions.

Built onto a private house, stove houses, as they used to be called, need to be isolated from other rooms with either well-sealed double-glazed doors, or a short corridor or glasshouse with an intermediate climate. The interior of such a conservatory must be

be re-created. Amongst the tropical foliage and blossom, butterflies and humming birds can flutter and whir, while in the centre of the building, a pool with warm-water fish and brightly coloured terrapins amongst the lotus leaves and flowers will complete the effect.

The Traditional Grotto

Occasionally old conservatories are decorated with ornaments made of shells and fossils, tufa, flint, and other geological curiosities. The idea comes from Italian Mannerist architecture and the grottos seen by English visitors to Italy from the eighteenth century onwards. Though these were usually constructed outside, they lend themselves particularly well to the decoration of garden rooms in which extraordinary fantasies can be assembled from bizarrely shaped rocks, dripping with ferns and mosses. These arrangements are ideal for a north-facing conservatory, where restricted light encourages lush growth. The Vict-

rigorously built to withstand the humidity, with moisture-resistant electrical wiring and fittings, plenty of paint or varnish over metalwork and wood, and with any exposed timber made of teak or iroko. Even with double-glazing, there will be condensation to live with, and wicker furniture, upholstery, and cushions will soon become mouldy. Nevertheless, for somebody with the resources and enthusiasm to build and maintain a conservatory having a constant temperature of 25°C (80°F) or more combined with humidifying equipment, a vast range of plants can be grown which would otherwise be impossible, and the lush, romantic style of a Victorian palm house may

LEFT *An unusually well-preserved Victorian fernery at the Morris Arboretum Conservatory in Philadelphia. In quite a small space, a woodland walk has been created, complete with a ferny dell, moss-covered rocky slopes, and a rustic bridge, set amongst large tree ferns and cycads.*

RIGHT *A design for the interior of a large conservatory, made by glassing over the garden at the back of a city house. The main walls, decorated with a skirting board of pattenered tiles, set off a formal arrangement of jardinières and wicker furniture. In the foreground is a large, round stone fountain which could be bordered by potted plants. Behind the cast-iron screen is a densely planted border with climbers trained up a decorative trellis.*

If you have a large conservatory building, a pool may be irresistible, but remember there are many practical problems in constructing and maintaining a pond indoors.

orians hunted and propagated rare 'sports' of native ferns and completed the ferny dell with tree ferns and cycads. Grottos require little heat and have year-round appeal, as they are generally evergreen and not dependent on blossom for their effect, but they require high humidity and must be kept shaded, unless the building is well protected from the sun.

It can be surprisingly easy to make very attractive decorative panels on the walls of a conservatory or garden room using contrasting shells (even such ordinary ones as cockles, mussels, clams, and oysters) with small flints, limestone, or black anthractie. For a more ambitious scheme, columns can be added decorated with the same materials, ceilings vaulted with rows of oysters or mussels imitating the ribs of stonework, and still lifes created out of the more impressive shells, such as abalones, murex, coral, and fossil ammonites. A central pool with a fountain in the same style can be built, with the brick or concrete construction masked by a mosaic or stones and shells. Further decoration can be added by introducing small pieces of broken china, glass, slag, and non-precious gems. To go all the way and 'grottify' the entire interior, the plant pots and furniture could be decorated in the same way. An excellent example of such a room exists at Woburn Abbey, where the chairs have been carved from wood and silver-gilded to look as if they are made of giant, glistening clam shells.

PLANTING WITH STYLE

A smart city conservatory is more likely to be a well-furnished room with few plants in a cool, formal style. Well-shaped architectural plants in attractive tubs are correct for this; the best types are orange or lemon trees, with their pleasing shape, and evergreen leaves, pretty scented flowers, and decorative (and, with some varieties, edible) fruit. Other possibilities for this style of garden room are camellias or, if the room is warm, gardenias, tree terns and cycads, agapanthus, all sorts of palms, ficus, and strelitzia (its leaves are very attractive). A variety of looks can easily be created by bringing in a succession of plants during their flowering season. Fuchsias, standard marguerite

daisies, some varieties of chrysanthemums, roses – especially miniatures – large arum lilies and true lilies (particularly the variety *L. longiflorum*) are useful if the look of the conservatory is to change with the seasons in this way. In a cool conservatory in mid-winter when little else will be in flower introducing forced bulbs will give both colour and scent.

It is not easy to grow herbs successfully in the conservatory. Most herbs derive their flavour from the aromatic oils that develop in the leaves as a protection against direct sunlight, and these therefore have the strongest flavour grown in an open sunny position, rather than under glass. Nevertheless, some herbs will do well in a conservatory, where they have a longer growing season. Chives can be grown in a pot throughout the year and are pleasing to look at with their small, onion-type flowers, although their smell can be a disadvantage in a confined space. Mint can be grown in a larger pot and will do well providing it is kept moist, and the many different varieties – spearmint, apple mint, pineapple mint, ginger mint, orange mint – could be used to make an interesting, fragrant display. Chervil is easy to grow under glass, and dill and coriander (make sure the seeds are for plants grown for leaves rather than their seeds) are worth trying: all have distinctive flavours and are delicious in soups and salads.

Conservatories lend themselves particularly well to enjoyment of the rich scents that many flowers produce. A jasmine planted in a conservatory flowerbed will, in a year or two, produce thousands of white, scented flowers in late winter and early spring, and with the conservatory door open will deliciously scent the entire house. Many of the plants associated with conservatories

have a strong fragrance which in a closed room can be almost overpowering. These include oranges and lemons, white datura, gardenia, hoya, lilies, mandevilla, mimosa, and stephanotis. A varied selection of plants can provide a succession of scented blossom through most of the year. There are also lots of plants with leaves that give off scent when brushed in passing – so be careful in choosing where they go. These include lemon verbena, some geraniums, and ginger, which has a wonderful smell.

Conservatory plants should be well-grown specimens which will make an attractive display. Large, symmetrical, 'standard' grown subjects, such as citrus fruit, palms, and tree ferns, are best planted in substantial pots or tubs and, because of their size and weight, need to be thoughtfully positioned. Smaller plants, in containers, will need more attention and careful watering, but can easily be moved around. Grouped together on a table, plant stand, or wirework jar-

The appeal of a tropical pool beneath glass is undeniable. In this conservatory, an entire bay-end has been made into a pond by an enthusiastic water gardener.

dinière, they can be used to create an instant floral effect. Climbers are often the largest plants in a conservatory, and will effectively cover walls and provide floral interest on the roof, but do best planted in large containers or, preferably, borders. These, however, must be planned and constructed as part of the building, and need good drainage and damp-proofing to keep the surrounding floor and walls dry. Small shade plants, such as selaginellas, maidenhair ferns, or mind-your-own-business can be used to carpet the spaces between larger plants. Hanging baskets of ferns, chlorophytum, mother-of-

TOOLS AND EQUIPMENT

Very few special tools are required, and certainly few that would not already be possessed by somebody with a garden. A small and manoeuvrable wheelbarrow is essential, as are appropriate watering cans. A large-capacity can with a general-purpose rose is useful for routine watering, and a smaller can, of 5-litre (1-gallon) capacity, is helpful for reaching high plants or those at the back of a border. Fitted with a fine rose, this can also be used for spraying and watering seedlings. Apart from the usual plastic or traditional galvanized cans, attractive brass and painted ones can be bought. If the conservatory has lots of plants it is essential to have an inside tap with a hose. This should have an adjustable sprayer at the end, ideally on a metal stalk, capable of being adjusted from a jet to a fine mist, and the hose should be connected to the tap with a good-quality quick-fit device so that it can be easily disconnected and the hose coiled up when not required. Secateurs, a trowel, a 'ladies spade', and garden scissors will be needed, as well as a few buckets (galvanized steel is best), and a sieve for grading soil. A hammer and bradawl for fitting hooks, vine eyes, and screw eyes for fitting hanging baskets and training wires are helpful, and a pair of pliers and wire cutters will be needed to put up the training wires. Some form of sprayer would be very useful for 'damping down', and spraying for disease. A flexible stem and remote sprayer can be used to reach foliage which would otherwise be inaccessible. A collection of plant labels, ties, and twine will also be needed, as well as fertilizers, fungicides, and insecticides.

thousands, small climbers such as black-eyed Susan, or even convolvulus, provide an alternative to the all-too-familiar pelargoniums and lobelia. Wire, painted or galvanized, is the best material for baskets, which, apart from the usual half-round, can now be bought in lots of pretty shapes.

OPPOSITE *The central pavilion of the conservatory at Chiswick House, which has recently been restored. The building houses a fine collection of camellias, including the beautiful single, red variety on the right.*

8

GUIDE TO CONSERVATORY PLANTS

Most house plants are selected by growers for their modest size, ability to withstand large variations in temperature, and tolerance of shade, but in a conservatory a much wider range of bulbs, annuals, climbers, shrubs and herbaceous plants can be grown. At the end of this book there is a list of specialist works about growing plants under glass for those seeking comprehensive information about how to grow and propagate different types of plants, and about soil, disease, and pest control.

Below is a personal selection of plants suitable for the conservatory that are relatively easy to grow and are available from good garden centres, or specialist nurserymen, listed in the section at the end of this book.

The plants described here are mostly large, and include a good proportion of climbers for people starting a garden under glass. They can be supplemented with lots of smaller flowering and foliage plants; these can often be picked up in roadside plant shops or cultivated from cuttings.

Abutilon Fast growing shrubs from South America, easy to grow in a border or large pots. There are many hybrids available in different colours, some of which have the advantage of flowering for most of the year. *A. striatum* 'Thompsonii' has orange flowers and interesting mottled-green and yellow foliage, and *A.* 'Nabob' has beautiful dark red flowers.

Acacia (wattle or mimosa) A group of trees and shrubs from Australia, some of which make beautiful, large conservatory plants, with their feathery, grey-green leaves and scented yellow flowers which appear during the winter and early spring. *A. dealbata* (mimosa) has silvery leaves and golden flowers but is very vigorous and will need a large conservatory, with a border, in which it can be planted. Two varieties, which are good for pots, are *A. baileyana*, which is slightly later flowering, and *A. pravissima* with curious silvery, triangular leaves.

Acca sellowiana (pineapple guava) Also sold as the 'fruit salad' bush. This handsome evergreen shrub has exotic flowers, red and white, with crimson stamens, which are edible. It has glossy evergreen leaves, and does well in a pot, developing into a handsome evergreen shrub.

Adiantum (maidenhair fern) There are many species of this smallish fern, with its delicate bright-green fronds on glossy, brittle stalks, and many are ideal for filling in gaps between flowering plants and shrubs, as they like to be in dappled shade. They do best in a moist atmosphere, and most will need some warmth.

Agapanthus Although there are now quite hardy versions of the perennial tub plant, which can be grown outside in the south of England, the earlier *A. africanus* with deep-blue flowers, and broader strap-like leaves, is ideal for the conservatory. It is evergreen and provides attractive foliage inside during the winter, and can be put outside to flower in summer.

Aloysia triphylla (lemon verbena) Although this plant becomes a straggly bush unless well-pruned, it should be grown for its leaves, which have a wonderful lemon scent when crushed. They can be picked at the end of the summer, dried, and used for pot pourri.

Anthurium The commonly grown species has heart-shaped leaves on long stalks and striking wax-like white, pink or red flowers which are the shape of a painter's palette. It requires a tropical atmosphere with both warmth and humidity to do well.

Asplenium bulbiferum (mother fern) This evergreen fern from Australasia has shiny pale-green fronds and makes an attractive plant 60–90 cm (2–3′) across. A botanical curiosity, it develops little plantlets on the upper surface of its fronds, which can be removed and potted up very easily to make new plants.

Billbergia nutans (angel's tears) A South American plant which develops a mass of long, greyish leaves, from amongst which pink and green-blue flowers appear. It is easy to grow, requires no heat, and is readily available.

Bougainvillea These brightly coloured, bushy climbers will be familiar from the Mediterranean. Grown in a sunny conservatory, with some heat in the winter, and fed during the summer, they will produce masses of blossom. There are many varieties, single and double, pink, red and white.

Caladium bicolor (angel's wings) Much admired for their extraordinary, elegant, heart-shaped leaves, which are marbled and splashed with green, white, red and cream. They are grown from tubers and reach about 37 cm (15″) high, but beware, they only like a high temperature, humidity and shade, and will not tolerate being chilly.

Camellia Although more often grown as garden plants, they are worth growing in pots, so that they can be brought into the conservatory in autumn to flower early in the new year. They are often seen in old conservatories, planted in the ground, where they have grown up to the roof. Remember that, if you grow them permanently indoors, they must be kept cool and moist during the summer. There are hundreds of varieties to choose from.

Citrus (oranges, lemons, grapefruits, mandarins and calamondins) These are some of the best plants for the conservatory with their shiny, evergreen leaves, scented white flowers, and colourful fruits. They are unusual in having both fruit and flowers on the bush at the same time. To do well, citrus need a constant temperature with plenty of light, careful watering and regular feeding during the growing season. *C. limon* 'Meyer' is one of the easiest citrus plants to grow and flowers almost continuously. *C. mitis*, the calamondin orange, does particularly well in pots, and produces miniature oranges all year round, which though rather sharp, can be used to make delicious marmalade. Sweet oranges, grapefruit, limes and mandarins can all be grown in a conservatory, but it is important to buy grafted plants, rather than grow them from pips.

Clivia Handsome plants, with arching, deep-green, strap-like leaves, producing bright orange-red flowers in early spring. They flower best when allowed to become pot bound, and should be fed well into the autumn.

Cobaea scandens (cup-and-saucer plant) This rampant climber will cover the inside of the conservatory roof in one season (and probably the outside as well, if allowed). It produces masses of bellflowers, which start green and gradually turn purple. It is best treated as an annual, and sown in March.

Cyperus papyrus Papyrus makes a wonderful plant for the conservatory pool as it likes to stand in water, or can be grown in a pot immersed in water. It has triangular green stalks, rising up to ten feet and topped by a mop of feathery leaves. It is easy to grow and quickly provides an impressive architectural effect.

Cyrtanthus speciosus (Scarborough lily) A bulb of the amaryllis family which provides colour in late summer with its bright, scarlet flowers. There are also forms with white, pink or bi-coloured flowers.

Cyrtomium see *Phanerophebia falacta*

Datura (angel's trumpets) The shrubs from this family produce huge trumpet-shaped flowers, which hang in quantity from beneath the leaves. An effective way of growing them is as a standard plant, so that the flowers will hang just above head-height. The white varieties have the advantage of richly scented flowers. *D. cornigera* 'knightii' (correctly *Brugmansia c.* 'knightii') is a double, impressive, white variety. *Brugmansia sanguinea*, with orange flowers, tipped with red, is less vigorous, and has a very long flowering period. There are also cream and lemon-yellow varieties. They can be grown in pots or in the ground, where they can reach 2.4 m (8′). It is a good idea to spray the plants with water as often as possible during the summer to ward off the red spider mite and white fly, to which they are prone. Beware, every part of the datura is poisonous.

Eriobotrya japonica (loquat) Although a loquat in a pot will not bear fruit, it should be grown as a foliage plant for its large, handsome leaves. It is also quick and easy to grow from seed, obtained from the fruit, which can often be found in green-grocers in late summer.

Eucalyptus (gum tree) Most are too large for conservatories, but there is a graceful, lemon-scented variety, *E. citriodora*, with golden-green leaves and a pinkish trunk, which will grow well in a tub.

Feijoa sellowiana see *Acca sellowiana*

Ferns A vast group of non-flowering, spore-bearing plants, a few of which are described separately. They include tiny, delicate, and feathery plants that live amongst rocks and dripping water, huge tree ferns, the extraordinary stags horn ferns, and even climbing species. Nearly all must have shade and humidity, although not necessarily heat, and are ideal for a north-facing conservatory, where they do well, grouped together to conserve moisture. Some do well in hanging baskets, such as *Nophrolepis exalta*, or *Davallia canariensis*, the hare's foot fern, named after its extraordinary, furry runners which will develop over the side of the basket, and from which new

The magnificent, restored Victorian conservatory at Ettington Park Hotel, near Stratford-upon-Avon, Warwickshire.

shoots appear. *Platycerium bifurcatum* (stag's horn fern) can also be grown in a basket, or on a block of wood against a wall (it is epiphytic), and produces apple-green antler fronds, which in the case of *P. superbum* will reach 90 cm (3′) or more in length. *Osmunda regalis* (the royal fern), though a hardy indigenous plant, makes a fine display, potted up and grown in a conservatory, under glass. Selaginallas, strictly speaking not ferns, have delicate fronds, and a creeping habit; they are ideal for spreading over rocks, or bare patches in corners, or under staging.

Ficus carica (common fig) In addition to their fruit, their large leaves make them an excellent foliage plant

during the summer. Although traditionally planted against a wall, they can also be grown in pots, as standards, and like this will fruit well, as they require a restricted root run. There are many varieties and these are readily available.

Gardenia jasminoides This plant with its wonderful glossy, green leaves, and highly scented double, creamy-white flowers, is irresistible. However it rarely continues to keep up appearances when taken into the conservatory. It likes a warm, moist, tropical atmosphere, and will beneft from being sprayed with water as often as possible during the summer. Unless you live in a soft-water district, always water with rainwater.

Gloriosa rothschildiana An exotic climber which grows by supporting itself with tendrils from the ends of its leaves. It develops lily-like flowers with red and yellow crinkly petals, and will reach 1.8 or 2.1 m (6 or 7′), grown from tubers planted in March in a warm conservatory.

Hardenbergia violacea An evergreen climber from Australia with deep violet, pea-shaped flowers, which appear between January and April. There is also a pink variety,

Hibiscus In Hawaii, where it is the national flower, raw flowers are eaten to aid digestion. Hibiscus are wonderful for pots in a conservatory, as long as they are cut back after flowering in the autumn to prevent them from becoming straggly. There are many varieties to choose from.

Hoya carnosa (wax plant) Another attractive, evergreen climber for the conservatory, with succulent, shiny, pointed leaves. *H. carnosa* has fragrant, pinkish-white flowers which hang in umbels, and develop a dew of nectar. Easy to grow, it can be trained up and along wires, beneath the roof, so the flowers can be seen from below. *H. bella*, a dwarf variety, is ideal for hanging baskets, as it likes to trail.

Ipomoea (morning glory) Vigorous twiners with quantities of large, trumpet-shaped flowers, which each last for a day. *I. rubro-caerulea* 'Heavenly Blue' is the fast-growing, annual climber with sky-blue flowers easily sown from seed in April. *I. learii* (the blue dawn flower) is a beautiful perennial twiner, and has deep-blue flowers which gradually fade during the day to pale mauve, and flowers profusely from June to October, but must be kept under control.

Jasminum (jasmine) Evergreen climbers, ideal for the conservatory. Easy to grow, trouble-free, and producing clouds of sweet, scented flowers. Some like tropical conditions, such as the beautiful *J. sambac*, gardenia-like, with large, double-white flowers and glossy, dark-green leaves. *J. polyanthum*, the most popular, is almost hardy, and has masses of white flowers, opening from rosy-pink buds which appear in late winter. *J. azoricum* likes to be a little warmer, but the white flowers are larger, and the flowering period longer.

Lapageria (Chilean bellflower) The national flower of Chile, named after the Empress Josephine (de la Pagerie) is

Design for an aquarium in a Victorian Gothic conservatory.

one of the most beautiful climbers available. It has waxy, bell-shaped, deep-pink flowers (there is also a white variety available) which are produced nearly all year round, and dark-green, leathery leaves. However, it is not an easy plant to grow. The soil must be evenly moist, completely lime-free, and the conditions cool and shady. Although best grown in the conservatory bed with a wall to climb, it can also be planted in a pot.

Lilies Most garden lilies also do well in pots and provide colour, scent, and interest in the conservatory, or on the terrace outside from early summer to autumn. Favourite lilies for pots are *L. auratum* (gold ray of Japan) and *L. candidum* (madonna lily), with lots of

pure, waxy, white trumpet-shaped flowers. *L. regale* is particularly easy to grow, and has white flowers with pale purple on the outside; it is heavenly scented. It is best to grow them outside in a sheltered place, and bring them in to flower.

Lippia citriodora see *Aloysia triphylla*

Mandevilla (also known as *Dipladenia*) Vigorous South American climbers for a large conservatory, where they should be grown in a bed and trained up into the rafters. *M. suaveolens* has creamy-white, funnel-shaped flowers which are deliciously fragrant. *M. × amabilis* 'Alice du pont' is evergreen and the large flowers are a glowing pink.

Musa (banana) Unless you have a hot-house, a banana plant is unlikely to produce edible fruit but the tree-like plants with their enormous leaves give a tropical atmosphere to any conservatory. Often available in garden centres: look for *M. basjoo* from Japan, and the Ethiopian *M. ensete* which both do well in cool conservatories.

Nerium oleander There are lots of varieties of these familiar Mediterranean shrubs, varying from white to dark red, or yellow, some single and some double. Grow them in tubs or pots, stand them outside during the summer, and water and feed them copiously from May to September, but very little during the winter, and prune them hard back in November.

Orchids As most orchids are epiphytic, and in the wild mostly grow on the branches of trees, to cultivate them is a specialised task. However, there are some which are easy to grow in a conservatory. Cymbidiums, for example, need little heat, as long as they have good light and plenty of ventilation, and you should be able to get them to flower again the following year.

Palms A large group of plants, ranging in size from small Mexican parlour palms 60 cm (2′) high, to large, mainly tropical trees. Greatly admired by the Victorians and grown for their architectural effect in conservatories, they have enjoyed a revival, and a much larger range for varying conditions is now available from specialist nurseries.

Pandorea jasminoides (the bower plant) A rare evergreen climber, producing clusters of trumpet-shaped flowers which are delicate, pale pink, with a crimson throat, and, with careful watering and feeding, can be grown in pots. *P. pandorana* (wonga wonga vine) is similar, with shiny, deep green foliage, and large pendular sprays of creamy-white trumpet flowers which are spotted with purple throughout the summer.

Passiflora (passionflowers) The early missionaries saw these unique flowers as a symbol of Christ's Passion. A number of species, with varying hardiness of this vigorous, tendril-climbing plant, are suitable for the conservatory. The commonly grown garden *P. caerulea*, with blue and white flowers, will need pruning hard back after flowering. *P. edulis* has greeny

flowers and produces the passion fruit, but needs to be warmer. *P. antioquiensis* has shocking pink flowers, and *P. amethystina*, with fine, elegant stems, is blue-purple. If you have a large conservatory, and keep it warm, *P. quadrangularis* (the giant grenadilla) is a must. This robust climber has edible fruit, which can weigh up to a pound, and fragrant red, white and purple flowers.

Pelargonium (commonly referred to as geranium) The scented-leaved geraniums from South Africa are attractive pot plants for any conservatory, providing fragrance and beautiful foliage throughout the year. *P.* 'Prince of Orange' has a strong citrus smell. *P.* × *fragrans* has grey leaves and smells of nutmeg, and *P. tomentosum* has large velvet, green-grey leaves, and a strong peppermint scent. There are many, many more and, easy to grow from cuttings, it is fun to make a collection.

Phanerophebia falacta (holly fern) A useful fern for the conservatory, as it doesn't seem to mind a dry atmosphere. It has large leathery leaves which are dark-green, serrated and shiny, and will grow to about 60 cm (2′) high.

Plumbago aunculata This must be the favourite climbing shrub for the conservatory. The unique clusters of slightly greyish-blue, phlox-like flowers last for many weeks in summer. Like most climbers it does best planted out, but will grow well in a tub against a wall. The white form *P. alba* is also easily obtainable.

Prostranthera rotundifolia (Australian mint bush) A delightful, late-winter flowering shrub, with aromatic foliage and masses of lilac blossom. It will flower when it is only 40 cm (18″) high, although ultimately it will reach 1.8 or 2.1 m (6 or 7′).

Roses Although roses are usually thought of as garden plants, there are some that are slightly tender and suitable for growing under glass such as *R.* 'Maréchal Niel', a climber, with creamy, yellow flowers, coppery-green foliage and a wonderful scent. If you have a large coolish conservatory, then *R. banksiae* 'Lutea', which can reach 6 m (20′), producing large cascading trusses of small pale yellow double flowers in late spring, may be worth growing or *R.* 'La Follette' which has deep, pink flowers, and abundant foliage.

Sparmannia africana (South African lime) You will need space to accommodate this fast-growing, flowering shrub with large, soft, light-green leaves. The flowers which are produced in clusters during the early spring are white with showy yellow stamens. It needs annual repotting and cutting back each spring to control its size. Don't throw the cuttings away, pot them up, and in one season you will have a 90 cm (3′) bushy plant.

Stephanotis floribunda (Madagascar jasmine) Most people will have seen stephanotis in garden centres grown as a pot plant, trained over a hoop of wire, and flowering at any time during the year. It is, however, a very beautiful evergreen, twining climber with fragrant, waxy, white flowers, which naturally appear in clusters during the summer. To thrive it needs a minimum temperature of 18°C (68°F), a moist atmosphere, and shade from direct sun.

Strelitzia reginae (the bird of paradise flower) This South African plant with palmy leaves and really exotic, purple, bird-shaped flowers is surprisingly easy to grow, though it will take some years to flower. Grown in a large tub in a sunny place, it will eventually form a clump, and flower very reliably once established.

Tetrastigma voinieranum (chestnut palm) If you have space and need to cover an area quickly this rampant, tropical climber is ideal. It has brown hairy branches, coiled, wiry tendrils and enormous chestnut-shaped leaves. It does like a constant warm temperature and benefits from being sprayed with water in summer.

Tibouchina semidecandra This evergreen flowering shrub from Brazil with velvety, luminous, royal purple flowers produced continuously for many months, must be included in the conservatory plant collection. It eventually reaches 3 m (10′), unless pruned to keep it to a reasonable size, and benefits from being grown against a wall where it can be supported.

Tree ferns Wonderful shuttlecocks of enormous green fronds, unfurling from a woody trunk. There are many species. *Dicksonia antarctica* is the most commonly available. It requires no heat and its trunk will generally reach 1.8 or 2.1 m (6 or 7′) under glass, but it does need a moist semi-shaded position in an airy glasshouse.

Vallota see *Cyrtanthus speciosus*

Vitis (grapevine) It is very satisfying to be able to pick a bunch of delicious, ripe home-grown grapes, but to grow them successfully under glass will restrict the usefulness of a conservatory. They like to be cold during the winter, and should ideally have their roots outside the conservatory, and require lots of space, and it should be remembered that their branches do not look attractive in winter. It is, however, now possible to buy ready-trained, standard plants in a number of varieties which can be grown in pots and produce good quality fruit. *V.* 'Black Hamburgh' is a popular and reliable grape for a container, and *V.* 'Muscat of Alexandria' is an excellent white grape.

Zantedeschia aethiopica (arum lily) The familiar funeral lily has beautiful waxy, white funnel-shaped flowers, up to 15–20 cm (6–8″) long, and glossy arrowhead leaves 60–90 cm (2–3′) high. It does well in pots, and may flower as early as Christmas.

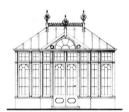

LISTINGS

Conservatory designers and builders

AMDEGA LTD
Faverdale, Darlington
County Durham DL3 0PW
Tel. 0325 468 522
Standard designs. Victorian style white-painted cedar conservatories.

BARTHOLOMEW CONSERVATORIES
277 Putney Bridge Road
London SW15 2PT
Tel. 081 785 7263
Traditional designs. Painted timber, natural oak or other hardwoods.

DOROTHEA LTD
Pearl House, Hardwick Street, Buxton
Derbyshire SK17 6DH
Tel. 0298 79121
Cast-iron conservatories, verandas, columns, fountains, and furniture.

HALL'S CONSERVATORIES
Church Road, Paddock Wood, Tonbridge
Kent TN12 6EU
Tel. 0892 834 444
Standard designs. Good-quality moderately priced bay-ended cedar or painted conservatories.

MARSTON & LANGINGER CONSERVATORIES LTD
192 Ebury Street
London SW1W 8UP
Tel. 071 823 6829
Painted hardwood conservatories, all individually designed. Full construction service, interior decoration and planting schemes. Blinds. Conservatory showroom.

OAKLEAF CONSERVATORIES
Unit 5, Kettlestring Lane, Clifton Common Industrial Park
York YO3 8XS
Tel. 0904 690 401
Moderately priced painted-cedar conservatories to order.

ROOM OUTSIDE LTD
Goodwood Gardens, Goodwood, Nr Chichester
West Sussex PO18 0QB
Tel. 0243 776 563
Solidly constructed made-to-order conservatories.

VALE GARDEN HOUSES
Melton Road, Harlaxton, Nr Grantham
Lincolnshire NG32 1HQ
Tel. 0476 64433
Combination of extruded- and cast-aluminium and wood. Made to order from standard components. Full construction service.

Conservatory garden designer and plant suppliers

ARCHITECTURAL PLANTS
Cooks Farm, Nuthurst, Horsham
West Sussex RH13 6LH
Tel. 0403 891 772
As the name says. A number are suitable for the conservatory.

BURNCOOSE NURSERIES
Gwennap, Redruth
Cornwall TR16 6BJ
Tel. 0209 861 112
Conservatory and hardy plants.

CHELSEA GARDENER, THE
125 Sydney Street
London SW3 6NR
Tel. 071 352 5656
Plants and a good selection of seeds, as well as books, furniture and pots.

CLIFTON NURSERIES
5a Clifton Villas, Warwick Avenue
London W9 2PH
Tel. 071 289 6851
Conservatory and hardy plants, plus new and period garden furniture and antiques.

HARDY EXOTIC PLANTS
Trebah Nursery, Mawnan Smith, Nr Falmouth
Cornwall TR11 5JZ
Tel. 0326 250 915
Despite the name, many conservatory plants.

GERNAEY, SUSAN
36 Salcott Road
London SW11 6DE
Tel. 071 223 1195
Landscape gardener and conservatory designer.

NATURAL PEST CONTROL LTD
Yapton Road, Barnham, Bognor Regis
West Sussex PO22 0BQ
Tel. 0243 553 250
Natural predators for controlling glasshouse pests.

PALM CENTRE, THE
563 Upper Richmond Road West
London SW14 7ED
Tel. 081 876 1193
Wonderful selection of conservatory palms.

ROYAL HORTICULTURAL SOCIETY GARDEN
Wisley, Woking
Surrey GU23 6QB
Tel. 0483 224 234
Plant information service and conservatory plant shop.

SYON PARK GARDEN CENTRE
Syon Park, Brentford
Middlesex TW8 8AG
Tel. 081 568 0134
Wide range of plants, including many tender subjects. Pots and furniture.

TREWIDDEN ESTATE NURSERY
Trewidden Gardens, Penzance
Cornwall TR20 8TT
Tel. 0736 62087
Unusual range of tender plants.

Floors, blinds, and other fittings

BISQUE DESIGNER RADIATORS
244 Belsize Road
London NW6 4BT
Tel. 071 328 2225
Radiators and heating consultants.

CADDICKS CLAY PRODUCTS LTD
1 Russell Chambers, The Piazza
London WC2E 8AA
Tel. 071 240 8738
Manufacturers of traditional clay tiled floors for conservatories and rope-pattern and other flower-border edging tiles.

CLIMATE CONTROLS LTD
La rue des Frenes, St Martin's, Guernsey
Channel Islands
Tel. 0481 37691
Automatic ventilation-control equipment

DOMUS
33 Parkgate Road
London SW11 4NP
Tel. 071 223 5555
Granite, terracotta, and Italian marble floors.

FIRED EARTH
Twyford Mill, Oxford Road, Adderbury
Oxfordshire OX17 3HP
Tel. 0295 812 088
Large range of terracotta and other tiles

T & W IDE LTD
Glasshouse Fields
London E1 9HY
Tel. 071 790 2333
All kinds of glass, including leaded lights and bent glass.

H & R JOHNSON TILES LTD
Highgate Tile Works Brownhills Road, Tunstall
Stoke-on-Trent
Staffordshire ST6 4JX
Tel. 0782 575 575
Geometric and encaustic floor tiles.

PARIS CERAMICS
583 King's Road
London SW6 2EH
Tel. 071 371 7778
Old French floors, mosaic tiles.

PLYGLASS PLC
Cotes Park Industrial Estate, Somercotes
Derbyshire DE55 4PL
Tel. 0773 520 000
Safety-glass and double-glazing manufacturer.

STAR CERAMICS
75 Lower Sloane Street
London SW1W 8DA
Tel. 071 259 9300
Conservatory floor tiles.

TECHNICAL BLINDS LTD
Old Town Lane, Wooburn
    Town, Nr High Wycombe
Buckinghamshire HP10 OPN
Tel. 06285 30511
External Venetian blinds for roofs.
    Manual, or fully automatic
    with solar control.

TIDMARSH & SONS
1 Laycock Street
London N1 1SW
Tel. 071 226 2261
Blind manufacturers.

TOWNSENDS
1 Church Street
London NW8 8EE
Tel. 071 724 3746
Antique and reproduction stained
    and cut glass.

Furniture

ANDREW CRACE DESIGNS
Bourne Lane, Much Hadham
Hertfordshire SG10 6ER
Tel. 0279 842 685
Wooden furniture and planters,
    gazebos.

CHATSWORTH CARPENTERS
Building Yard, Chatsworth
    Park, Chatsworth, Bakewell
Derbyshire DE45 1PP
Tel. 0246 582 242
Traditional timber furniture for
    garden or conservatory.

CONRAN SHOP, THE
Michelin House
    81 Fulham Road
London SW3 6RD
Tel. 071 589 7401
Conservatory and garden
    furniture.

INDOOR ROOM, THE
Stratton Audley Hall,
    Stratton Audley
Oxfordshire OX6 9BG
Tel. 0869 278 256
Antique conservatory furniture.

ROBIN EDEN
Pickwick End, Corsham
Wiltshire SN13 OJB
Tel. 0249 713 335
Regency-pattern hoop-back seats.
    Traditional wirework furniture.

WHITEHILL LTD
85 Leonard Street
London EC2A 4QS
Tel. 071 729 6633
Reproduction cast-iron urns,
    fountains, and furniture.

Statuary and miscellaneous

ANTHONY DE GRAY GARDENS
1 Cambridge Road
London SW11 4RT
Tel. 071 228 8808
High-quality handmade traditional
    trellises and gazebos.

ARCHITECTURAL CERAMICS
120 Faircharm Trading Estate
London SE8 3DX
Tel. 081 692 7287
Classical ceramic fountain statues,
    pots, and urns. Stock items and
    commissions.

ARCHITECTURAL HERITAGE
Taddington Manor,
    Taddington, Nr Cutsdean,
    Cheltenham
Gloucester GL54 5RY
Tel. 038 673 414

ARTECH
Unit 15, Burmarsh
    Workshops, Marsden Street
London NW5 3JA
Tel. 071 428 2181
Trellises, planters, and wooden
    garden furniture.

BARRIE QUINN ANTIQUES
3–4 Broxholme House, New
    King's Road
London SW6 4AA
Tel. 071 736 4747
Wire jardinières and hanging
    baskets.

CROWTHER OF SYON LODGE
Busch Corner, London Road,
    Isleworth
Middlesex TW7 5BH
Tel. 081 560 7978
Lots of antique urns, statuary,
    fountains, and garden furniture.

HADDONSTONE LTD
The Forge House, East Haddon
Northamptonshire NN6 8DB
Tel. 0604 770 711
Cast-stone urns, fountains,
    statuary, architectural steps and
    sills, finials, and balustrades.

INCHBALD SCHOOL OF DESIGN, THE
32 Eccleston Square
London SW1V 1PB
Tel. 071 630 9011
Garden-design school.

RICHARD QUINNELL LTD
Oxshott Road, Leatherhead
Surrey KT22 OEN
Tel. 0372 375 148
All kinds of high-quality wrought-
    ironwork.

SEAGO
22 Pimlico Road
London SW1W 8LJ
Tel. 071 730 3223
Antique garden ornaments,
    statuary, fountains, and
    wrought-iron seating.

SOLOPARK LTD
The Old Railway Station
    Station Road
    Nr Pampisford
Cambridgeshire CB2 4HB
Tel. 0223 834 663
Architectural salvage, floors, rope
    flower-border edging, and new
    cast-ironware.

WALCOT RECLAMATION
108 Walcot Street, Bath
Avon BA1 5BG
Tel. 0225 444 404
Architectural salvage, including all
    conservatory components.

WHICHFORD POTTERY
Whichford, Nr Shipton-on-
    Stour
Warwickshire CV36 5PG
Tel. 060 884 416
Good range of designs and sizes of
    frostproof handmade pots.

Associations and Books

ACANTHUS ASSOCIATED
    ARCHITECTURAL PRACTICES
Voysey House, Barley Mow
    Passage
London W4 4PN
Tel. 081 995 1232
An association of conservation
    architects specializing in careful
    and appropriate additions and
    alterations to period houses.

CONSERVATORY ASSOCIATION, THE
Godwin House, George Street,
    Huntingdon
Cambridgeshire PE18 6BU
Tel. 0480 458 278
Trade association representing a
    number of conservatory
    manufacturers.

ENGLISH HERITAGE
23 Savile Row
London W1X 2HE
Tel. 071 734 6010
Established by the Department of
    the Environment as custodians
    of historically and
    architecturally important sites.
    Will provide conservation
    advice.

HEATING AND VENTILATION
    CONTRACTORS' ASSOCIATION
Esca House, 34 Palace Court
London W2 4JG
Tel. 071 229 2488
Helpful if you have a special
    problem outside the scope of
    general central-heating
    installers.

ROYAL INCORPORATION OF
    ARCHITECTS IN SCOTLAND, THE
15 Rutland Square, Edinburgh
Scotland EH1 2BE
Tel. 031 229 7205

ROYAL INSTITUTE OF BRITISH
    ARCHITECTS, THE
66 Portland Place
London W1N 4AD
Tel. 071 580 5533

ROYAL INSTITUTION OF CHARTERED
    SURVEYORS, THE
12 Great George Street
London SW1P 3AE
Tel. 071 222 7000

VICTORIAN SOCIETY, THE
1 Priory Gardens
London W4 1TT
Tel. 081 994 1019
Provide information on Victorian
    buildings and are consulted on
    Listed Buildings applications.

A Selected Bibliography

ABERCROMBIE, J., *The Hot House Gardener*, London, 1789.

AMERICAN GREENHOUSE MANUFACTURING COMPANY, *American Greenhouses*, Chicago, n.d.

BIRD, ANTHONY, *Paxton's Palace*, London, Cassell, 1976.

BONIFACE, PRISCILLA, *The Garden Room*, London, HMSO, 1982.

BRITZ, BILLIE S., *The Greenhouse at Lyndhurst* (Research on Historic Properties Occasional Papers, no. 1), Washington, D.C., National Trust for Historic Preservation, Preservation Press, 1977.

CARTER, GEORGE, GOODE, PATRICK and LAURIE, KEDRUN, *Humphry Repton, Landscape Gardener*, Norwich, Sainsbury Centre for Visual Arts, 1982.

CHADWICK, G. F., *The Works of Sir Joseph Paxton*, London, The Architectural Press, 1961.

DEFOREST, ELIZABETH KELLAM, *Gardens and Grounds at Mount Vernon*, Mount Vernon, Virginia, Mount Vernon Ladies Association of the Union, 1982.

DICKSON, ELIZABETH (ed.), *The English Garden Room*, London, Weidenfeld and Nicolson, 1986.

DIESTELKAMP, EDWARD, 'The Conservatories and Hot-Houses of Richard Turner', pub. in *Historic Greenhouses and Kew*, Kew, Royal Botanic Gardens, 1982.
'The Design and Building of the Palm House, Royal Botanic Gardens, Kew', *Journal of Garden History*, 2 (3).

ELLIOTT, DR BRENT, *Victorian Gardens*, London, Batsford, 1986.

FAWKES, FRANK A., *Horticultural Buildings, their Construction Heating, Interiors, Fittings, etc.*, London 1881.

Gardeners Magazine, ed. J. C. Loudon.

GARNOCK, JAMIE, *Trellis*, London, Thames and Hudson, 1991.

GLOAG, JOHN, *Mr Loudon's England*, Newcastle-upon-Tyne, Oriel Press 1970.
and BRIDGEWATER, DEREK, *A History of Cast Iron in Architecture*, London, Allen and Unwin, 1948.

HEPPER, NIGEL, *Plant Hunting for Kew*, London, HMSO, 1989.

HIBBERD, JAMES SHIRLEY, *The Amateur's Greenhouse and Conservatory*, London, Croombridge and Sons, 1875.
The Fern Garden, London, 1870.
Rustic Adornments for Homes of Taste, London, Driffield, 1856.

HIX, JOHN, *The Glass House*, London, Phaidon, 1974.

HYAMS, EDWARD, *Capability Brown and Humphry Repton*, London, Dent, 1971.

JEKYLL, GERTRUDE, *Garden Ornament*, London, Country Life and George Newnes, 1918.

JONES, BARBARA, *Follies and Grottoes*, London, Constable, 1953.

KOHLMAIER, G., and VON SARTORY, B., *Houses of Glass*, Cambridge, Mass. and London, MIT Press, 1986.

KOPPELKAMM, STEFAN, *Glasshouses and Wintergardens of the Nineteenth Century*, St Albans, Granada, 1981.

LANGLEY, BATTY, *Gothic Architecture Improved*, London, 1742.

LEIGHTON, ANN, *American Gardens in the Eighteenth Century*, 'For Use or for Delight', Amherst, The University of Massachusetts Press, 1986.

LEMMON, KENNETH, *The Covered Garden*, London, Museum Press, 1962.

LEUCHARS, ROBERT B., *A Practical Treatise on the Construction, Heating and Ventilation of Hot-houses, etc.*, Boston, John P. Jewett and Company, 1851.

LOUDON, J. C., *The Encyclopaedia of Gardening*, London 1822 and 1850.
The Greenhouse Companion, London 1824.
Sketches of Curvilinear Hothouses, London, 1818.

MACDOUGALL, ELIZABETH B. (ed.), *John Claudius Loudon and the Early Nineteenth Century in Great Britain*, Dumbarton Oaks Colloquium on the History of Landscape Architecture, VI, Dumbarton Oaks, 1980.

MACFARLANE, WALTER, *Macfarlane's Architectural Ironwork*, Glasgow, 1922. Macfarlane's Castings, Vols I, II and III.

MCGRATH, RAYMOND, and FROST, A. C., *Glass in Architecture and Decoration*, London, The Architectural Press, 1937.

M'INTOSH, CHARLES, *The Greenhouse, Hot-House and Stove*, London, 1838.

Magazine of Botany, ed. Joseph Paxton.

MESSENGER AND COMPANY LIMITED, *Conservatory and Greenhouse Catalogue*, Loughborough and London, 1900s.

MILLER, PHILIP, *Decimus Burton, A Guide to the Exhibition of his Work*, London, Building Centre Trust, 1981.

MINTER, SUE, *The Greatest Glasshouse*, London, HMSO, 1990.

MOORE, PATRICIA, *Margam Orangery*, Glamorgan, Glamorgan Archive Service, 1986.

PAPWORTH, J. B., *Hints on Ornamental Gardening*, London, 1823.
Rural Residences, London, 1818.

RANDALL, COLVIN, L., 'Longwood, History of the Conservatories', unpublished material, 1987.

REES, YVONNE, and PALLISER, DAVID, *Conservatory Gardening*, Swindon, Crowood, 1990.

REPTON, HUMPHRY, *Fragments on the Theory and Practice of Landscape Gardening*, London, 1816.
Observations on the Theory and Practice of Landscape Gardening, London, 1803.

RICHARDSON & CO., Catalogue, n.d.

ROWAN, ALASTAIR, *Garden Buildings*, Feltham, Country Life, 1968.

SEDDON, GEORGE, and BICKNELL, ANDREW, *The Complete Guide to Conservatory Gardening*, London, Collins, 1986.

STRAHAN, EDWARD, *Mr. Vanderbilt's House and Collection*, 2 vols, Boston, New York, Philadelphia, George Barrie, 1883–4.

TAFT, LEVI RAWSON, *Greenhouse Construction, A Complete Manual*, New York, Orange Judd, 1894.

TALLACK, J. C., *The Book of the Greenhouse*, New York and London, J. Lane, 1908.

TANNER, OGDEN, *Garden Rooms: Greenhouse, Sunroom and Solarium Designs*, New York, Linden Press/Simon and Schuster, 1986.

TAYLOR, JASMINE, *Conservatories and Garden Rooms*, London, Macdonald, 1985.

THOMPSON, FRANCIS, *Chatsworth: A Short History*, London, Country Life, 1951.

THOMPSON, ROBERT, *The Gardener's Assistant*, Blackie and Son, 1878.

TODD, GEORGE, *Plans, Elevations and Sections of Hot-Houses, Greenhouses, etc.*, York, 1807.

TRESSIDER, JANE, and CLIFF, STAFFORD, *Living under Glass*, London, Thames and Hudson, 1986.

VAN DEN MUIJZENBERG, DR ERWIN W. B., *A History of Greenhouses*, Wageningen, Institute for Agricultural Engineering, 1980.

VANCE, MARY, *Garden Rooms and Greenhouses: A Bibliography*, Architectural Series A-1042, Monticello, Illinois, Vance Bibliographies, 1983.

WOODS, MAY and WARREN, ARETE, *The Glasshouse*, London, Aurum Press, 1988.

Index

Numbers in *italics* refer to illustration captions.